RHYMING HISTORY

The Story of England in Verse

RHYMING HISTORY
The Story of England in Verse

by Colin Wakefield

Illustrations by John Partridge

VOLUME FIVE: 1660 – 1685

Charles the Second and the Restoration

DHP
Double Honours Publications

RHYMING HISTORY
The Story of England in Verse

VOLUME FIVE: 1660 – 1685
Charles the Second and the Restoration

First published in 2015 by Double Honours Publications.

ISBN 978-0-9570120-4-2

Double Honours Publications

Email: info@rhyminghistory.co.uk
Website: www.rhyminghistory.co.uk
Twitter: @Rhyming_History

Printed and bound by Short Run Press, Exeter

AUTHOR'S NOTE

This is Volume Five of our *Rhyming History* (still in the writing), which will eventually stretch from Julius Caesar's invasion of Britain in 55BC to the present day.

Volume Six (James the Second – the Forgotten King) will also be published in 2015, with subsequent volumes appearing annually. All published volumes are available for sale through the website and selected retailers.

These books of verse are intended for those who want to learn about our history, but in not too solemn a way. I hope they will also appeal to a wider audience, students and historians, and those who simply enjoy reading verse.

Spellings from original sources have been modernised.

John Partridge has again provided witty and entertaining illustrations to accompany the text, for which I am as ever most grateful.

My special thanks are due to Jonathan Dowie for his detailed preparation of the text and for mastery of the website. I am also most grateful to Chris Moss for his help with the cover, to Stan Pretty and Philip Davies for their advice on the text, and to Michael Callahan and Chris Wakefield for their continued support.

Please visit our website for updates on future volumes of the *History*, and for news of live performances of the verse.

www.rhyminghistory.co.uk

Colin Wakefield – March 2015

Charles the Second and the Restoration

CHARLES THE SECOND (1660 – 1685)

England, 1660. Drift, stagnation,   **1660**
Exhaustion, disillusion, frustration…
A poor, divided, dispirited nation.

Oliver Cromwell had struggled, but failed.
Collapse was averted; muddle prevailed.
Then General Monck, of the cool, clear head,
Stepped into the breach. In Oliver's stead,
Enter King Charles. The Republic was dead.

Like magic it happened. Restoration:
Welcome relief! A crumbling nation
(Sick to the stomach of mind-numbing rules
Dictated by Cromwell's cronies, the fools)
Was more than prepared for a change of ways.
A return, in short, to the 'good old days'.

The King's arrival

So it was, on the 29th of May,
England's nightmare ended. I have to say,
The coincidence of the King's birthday,
His thirtieth, did lend a tender touch –
Not in the end that it mattered that much.
If books that I've read are to be believed,
A rapturous welcome the King received.
Embraced by his subjects with open arms,
Charles remarked wittily (one of his charms),
He'd bumped into so many friends that day
It was clearly his fault he'd stayed away.

He was kidding, of course. A long exile
Left him kicking his heels. Life was futile,
Boring, a waste – so deeply frustrating,
Living on credit, watching and waiting.

Rhyming History

The French extended a welcome of sorts,
But Oliver Cromwell (he of the warts)
Was a force to be reckoned with. France,
In her wisdom, was taking no chance.
When it suited her best, young Charles was 'out'.
The Dutch would welcome him better, no doubt –
His cousins were big in Holland; but no:
When Oliver wooed them, Charles had to go.
I'm skipping ahead, but such was his fate.
The Stuarts were well past their sell-by date.

You might reckon, having inherited
The crown from his father, Charles merited
Better treatment. But hey, that's politics –
A nest of corruption and dirty tricks.

Early years

The young Prince enjoyed a golden childhood.
At his birth the signs spelt nothing but good,
Charting Venus high in the ascendant,
Bright star of Love. This 'superintendant'
(Venus, I mean) had much to answer for
As Charles grew up: mistresses by the score
And thirteen royal bastards (maybe more –
Not being present, I couldn't be sure).
'Old Rowley' was one scandalous nickname
Owned by the naughty King (such was his fame).
Rowley, before you all ask, was a horse,
A great stallion... Sorry to be coarse.

A sturdy baby, no doubt about that –
Enormous, in fact. For Charles was "so fat,"
Wrote his mother, Henrietta, the Queen,
"That I am ashamed". I find this obscene.
She had lost one babe just a year before,
A sickly child. Her complaint I abhor.

Charles the Second and the Restoration

His teeth appeared when he was four months old,
Just fancy that. And moreover, we're told,
His skin was olive and his hair jet black,
Colouring he kept in an age (alack)
When a fair complexion was all the rage –
Precisely why, it's not easy to gauge.
His father was short, his mother was small,
Yet Charles, as a man, was monstrously tall.
On his flight from Worcester, a fugitive,
The 'Wanted' posters described (as I live)
"A tall, dark man above two yards high" –
A giant for the time. One might ask why,
Or how, his parents produced such a chap.

Some sort of rare, genetical mishap?
Or (God forbid) hanky-panky? Not so.
It was foreign forebears, I'll have you know.
Two grandparents (both on his mother's side)
Were French and Italian. You decide.

Rhyming History

His Italian looks, swarthy and dark –
Look no further. Princess Anne of Denmark
Was his dad's mother (a bit of a fright).
So, although his *pater*'s stature was slight,
There was Scandinavian blood. In height,
In strength and in courage the great Danes score.

To complete the picture, grandparent four
Was King James, the son (and this I deplore)
Of Mary, Queen of Scots – thrice-married, mad,
Catholic, bonkers and thoroughly bad.
From the Scottish Queen, I'd hazard a guess,
Came his reckless streak. I have to confess
That it served Charles well, for it seems to me
That monarchs must have the capacity
For a modest dose of duplicity.
King Charles could behave quite disgracefully,
At home and away. All this we shall see.

Charles as a child, according to reports,
Was kind, good-natured, rarely out of sorts,
Generous, energetic and sporty –
And (as is healthy) frequently naughty.
When he turned eight, the Earl of Newcastle
Became his tutor. The little rascal
He drilled in the virtues of courtesy,
Mannerly conduct and civility.
Charles had less regard for bookish pursuits,
With scholarship one of his weaker suits.
He nevertheless showed intelligence,
A lively mind and a measure of sense.
Some, like Hyde (though evidence is hazy),
Grumbled that Charles inclined to be lazy.
Well, I ask you, what else would you expect –
A Prince in exile? How mean can you get?
Above all, perhaps, he was taught respect
(Newcastle again) for the fairer sex,
And a wizard he proved, *Carolus Rex*!

Charles the Second and the Restoration

The Civil War

Twelve-year-old Charles was at his father's side
When Civil War broke out. The regicide
Was seven years distant. Now who'd have thought,
In 1642, that the King, Court,
Lords and Bishops – all would be swept away,
The King foully murdered? On the day,
August the 22nd, that the King
Raised his standard at Nottingham, nothing
(I repeat, nothing) could have seemed less real
Than a royal defeat. The King's appeal
Lay in his divine right. His victory
Was assured, with the hand of history
To guide his campaign. It's no mystery,
In retrospect, why King Charles the First lost.
He squandered his edge, at terrible cost,
Through arrogance and generosity
(That's strange to say) – too 'soft' an enemy.
Return and take a look at Volume Three,
I urge you. It's all there, for goodness' sake.
The point, however, I should like to make
Is that young Charles, standing beside his dad,
Was primed for the best fun he'd ever had.

Just imagine the excitement! The thrill!
Both he and James were present at Edgehill
(Wee James was ten), which was fought to a draw,
The first pitched battle of the Civil War.
The two small Princes were under the care
Of Dr. William Harvey. Aware
(Or not, as it transpired) that the fighting
Was close, his book proved far more exciting.
Dr. Harvey was the famous medic
Who discovered what makes our bodies tick –
The circulation of the blood, all that.
William found battles boring, old hat,

So lost himself in his studies. A blast,
An almighty big one, woke him at last.
A great cannon ball landed by the Princes.
Lethal and deadly, it missed them by inches.

That wasn't the only escape that day.
After the Doctor had led them away
(Not before time) to a more secure spot,
They found themselves facing, like it or not,
A small contingent of enemy horse.
Retreat was the only option, of course,
But the valiant Prince was heard to shout,
"I fear them not!" There's no shadow of doubt
That, despite Charles getting his pistol out
(Which he did), he'd surely have breathed his last
Had a Royalist not intervened – and fast.

Shortly after Edgehill James asked his dad,
"When shall we go home?" The outlook was bad.
"We have no home," came the answer. How sad.

1644 was a dreadful year:
Defeat at Marston Moor. The thin veneer
Of divine right was now badly tarnished
As reality, stark and unvarnished,
Obliged the King to face the awful truth
Of total loss. Prince Charles, despite his youth,
Was despatched to take command (at fifteen)
Of the troops in the west. He was too green,
Of course, to be more than a figurehead,
But he stayed a year. It has to be said
That King Charles' motives in sending his son,
His heir, from his side caused surprise to none.
His own position was thus more secure.
Parliament couldn't 'show him the door'
(Euphemism, that), in spite of the war,
Whilst his son and heir was beyond their reach.

As it transpired, of course (sorry to preach),
It sure didn't stop them, in '49,
From chopping his head off. All very fine,
But at this stage, early in '45,
The royalist hopes were best kept alive
By the separation, sad as it was,
Of father and son – the sadder because,
As they took their leave in the wind and rain,
They were destined never to meet again.

Exile

In the wake of Prince Rupert's surrender
Of Bristol later that year (September)
The game was up. The King had urged his son
Since Naseby (a rout) to pack up and run.
But where? Anywhere but France, anywhere,
Urged Edward Hyde in a fit of despair.
The Prince's adviser, fussy but sound,
He agreed that Charles had to go to ground,

Rhyming History

But not in a Catholic country. No,
To Scotland or Ireland the Prince should go.
Contrary arguments raged to and fro,
Until Charles (the King) settled the matter.
Queen Henrietta (mad as a hatter,
And dangerous to boot, such was Hyde's view –
Catholic zealot, but what could he do?)
Welcomed her husband's choice of location.
France it was. It became her vocation
To keep her little boy under her thumb
Until (quite literally) kingdom come.

She failed. Charles kept to his father's edict,
Who ordered the Prince (he was fairly strict)
To abjure all superstitions of Rome
And stick to the pure religion of home,
The Protestant faith. It has to be said,
Although Charles the Second died in his bed,
He did die a Catholic. This we'll see:
A deathbed conversion. "Duplicity!"
Cry the cynics. "Horrid dishonesty!"
"Fiddlesticks!" I reply. For who are we
To judge a man's spirituality,
Be he King or pauper? Sheer vanity.
That said, it were simple insanity
To state his religious preference
To his wary subjects. Charles had more sense.

I digress. Of this there'll be more anon,
But by June '46 the Prince was gone –
His destination, France. Now aged sixteen,
He was quite a lad (you know what I mean).
Mature for his years (in every way),
He'd an eye for the ladies. Come what may,
The Prince's demeanour was light and gay.
While Hyde complained that he lived for the day,
Was idle and shallow, others averred
That grumpy Edward was being absurd.

Charles was an optimist. What's wrong with that?
A positive outlook? I'll eat my hat
The day that's a fault. For the Prince was strong,
Dynamic, resilient. Right from wrong
He was apt to confuse, in times of stress.
Frankly, dear reader, I couldn't care less.
The secret of Charles the Second's success
Lay in his ease, his wit and good humour.
A bit of a shit? Only a rumour.

France proved a huge disappointment, and how!
Deprived of status and forced to kowtow
To his cousin King Louis, eight years old,
And a prig to boot (or so we are told),
Charles was kept short (this just isn't funny)
Of favour, respect and ready money.
His mother, the Queen, had sold off her plate
And her gold to buy food, such was her fate.
Her court in exile, a sad little crew,
Was riven with factions. What could it do

9

Rhyming History

But bicker and quarrel the long day through?
The Prince found his comfort (well, wouldn't you?)
In idle diversions, frequent *amours* –
Boredom and lack of direction the cause.

His tutor in maths, believe it or not,
Was Thomas Hobbes. Although Charles was no swot,
He took to the study of geometry,
Mathematics and science. Hobbes, you see,
Inspired him. In his *Brief Lives*, John Aubrey
Describes how Hobbes would "draw lines on his thigh
"And also on the sheets, abed" (strange guy)
And sing aloud at night "for his health's sake".

Though doubtless he kept the neighbours awake,
I like the sound of Hobbes. He used to say –
We're informed by old Aubrey, anyway –
That had he read as much as other men
He would have known no more than they. So then,
He owned few books! It's my considered guess –
I've no proof at all, I have to confess –
That to Charles, in a life of idleness,
Thomas Hobbes was a boon. For such a man
As could pen the mighty *Leviathan*
Was the rarest of gems. That's just my view.

But the Prince took his lead. Anything new
In the field of physics (chemistry, too)
Engaged his interest – navigation,
Mechanics. Years later, the foundation
Of the Royal Society (it's true)
Was his inspiration. For King Charles knew –
As old monarchs go, he's one of the few –
That the fortune of any great nation,
Its future, depends on innovation,
Enquiry and experimentation.

Charles the Second and the Restoration

The fate of Charles the First

The news from abroad was causing alarm.
The King had surrendered, without a qualm,
To the Scots. Their patience quickly wore thin.
Today we'd call it political spin:
Plain bad faith's a far better term for it.
For Charles wore the poor Scots down bit by bit –
Not to be trusted, as simple as that.
So they turned him over, off their own bat,
To Parliament. That didn't last long.
The Army, whose plans were all going wrong,
Wrested the King from Parliament's grip.
Men had begun to ask, "What price, kingship?"

No one knew. Then, one damp November night,
Charles escaped. He fled to the Isle of Wight.
Poor chap, he got the most terrible fright.
The Guv'nor of Carisbrooke Castle there
Was Oliver Cromwell's kinsman. Despair…
Confusion… Charles had been sold a pup,
A prisoner (you couldn't make it up)
Of the Army now for the second time.
Quite bizarre! The plot for a pantomime!

Speaking (as we appear to be) of plots,
The King in secret contacted the Scots
(Can you believe?) with an invitation
To mount, on his behalf, an invasion
Of *his* kingdom, for *his* 'restoration'!
This lunacy, which shocks one to the core,
Resulted in the second Civil War.
That so much blood was prepared to be shed
By the King, to save his own stupid head,
Signalled to some he'd be better off dead.
Such was the view of one extreme faction
In the Army, who called for swift action.

11

Rhyming History

"That man of blood," they were dubbing the King.
These same men called him "to account". Nothing
(I repeat, nothing) could save him now. So,
How did they feel in France? They didn't know!
It's true. Communications were that slow.

When news eventually filtered through
Of the King's trial, what could the Prince do?
Less than nothing, alas, as it turned out.
Charles would have intervened, without a doubt,
To 'spring' his father from the Isle of Wight –
Plans were afoot, if I've understood right –
Had such a strategy proved practical.
The problems, though, were more than tactical.
Charles lacked the resources. He had left France
For Holland, handing himself a slim chance
Of launching a surprise naval attack
On the Isle of Wight. So, what held him back?
No ships! No Navy! No money! No men!
Prospects for victory? One out of ten.

It's the very fag-end of '48.
King Charles was moved from Carisbrooke. His fate
Was sealed, despatched to Hurst Castle (grim place –
Damp and forbidding, a perfect disgrace)
And thence to Windsor, pending his trial.

Young Charles was enjoying Christmas the while
At The Hague. Wretchedness wasn't his style.
Don't judge him too harshly. What could he do?
The King was in prison, that much he knew.
Some letters, in fact, he had just received
From Carisbrooke Castle. Charles was relieved.
His beloved father's words of advice
Were a comfort indeed. Let these suffice:
"If God gives you success," he wrote (with care),
"Use it humbly and far from revenge." There:
Sound words of wisdom for his son and heir.

The King's execution

At this stage Charles still didn't realise
What weeks later came as a rude surprise.
The King was to be tried, tried for his life –
Ill tidings that cut through Charles like a knife.
To kill a King! His heart was torn in two,
Not least since there was little he could do.
Louis of France wrote a letter. Big deal!
First cousin and fellow royal, you feel
He might have tried harder. A mere letter!
The Dutch, God bless 'em, did a bit better.

13

Rhyming History

They sent two reps over to remonstrate.
Sadly, though, it was already too late
By the time they arrived. They spent their breath.
King Charles the First had been sentenced to death.

The axe fell. Regicide brought no relief
To a divided state poleaxed with grief.
Long live the King! Long live the late King's son –
Prince Charles, now known to everyone
(Abroad, at least) as King Charles the Second.
Eleven long years of exile beckoned.

The late King's execution sent shock waves
Across Europe. The foul regicides (knaves,
Assassins) were abhorred and vilified.
Poor Cromwell received a pretty rough ride.
In time, though, he and his hated cohorts
Demonstrated a competence of sorts.
Foreign governments were quick to cement
New alliances, even if this meant
Turning their backs on the King in exile –
First the fickle French, and then the Dutch: vile.
Grand young Louis was cousin to the King;
Apparently this counted for nothing.
William of Orange (and then his son)
Were also kinsmen, when all's said and done,
To Charles: the elder, his brother-in-law;
The younger, his nephew. In time of war,
However, things fly out of the window.
Sorry to be glib, but this you should know.

It is hard not to be cynical, though.
What harm had poor Charles done to anyone?
A King with no crown? That's hardly much fun.
But was he depressed? Was Charles downhearted?
No! He'd fight back. He itched to get started.

Charles the Second and the Restoration

Friends and allies – the Irish and the Scots

The Scots had also lost their King; ditto
The Irish. Both people, I'll have you know,
Were livid not to have been consulted
In the matter of their King – insulted,
Indeed. As a possible launching pad
To muster a force to avenge his dad
And regain his stolen kingdom, Ireland
Was the young King's preference. Understand,
If you will, that Charles viewed with some alarm
The Presbyterian Scots. They lacked charm,
Warmth and humour, wit and humanity,
And might seek to impose (this we shall see)
Their religion upon him (strict and stern) –
A faith that Charles was reluctant to 'learn'.

Ireland, conversely, was a better bet,
A complex, divided country, and yet
Prepared to fight for the royalist cause
Under James Butler (worthy of applause),
The 12th Earl of Ormonde – a loyalist,
Anglo-Irish, and a staunch Royalist.

When it came to 'launching pads', however,
The new *régime* (mark now just how clever)
Was ahead of the game. Cromwell was sent,
By urgent order of Parliament,
To quell the Irish 'rebels'. This he did,
In savage style, until Ireland was rid,
Once and for all, of any illusion
Of an independent will. Confusion,
Conflict, hatred, division… these, sadly,
Were Cromwell's grim and deadly legacy;
And, as in time the villain discovered,
His reputation never recovered.

Rhyming History

Across the water (in Jersey, in fact)
Charles, with a caution that Oliver lacked,
Was biding his time when word filtered through
Of the Irish bloodbath. What could he do?
Little, it seemed – though he surely now knew
That Ireland was off the agenda. So,
He turned to the Scots! He'd give them a go!
To be frank, if Charles still wanted a voice,
He'd have to succumb. He hadn't much choice.

But Scottish support was won at a price.
The necessitous King was forced (not nice)
To subscribe to their wretched Covenant.
Such pressure was wilful and ignorant.
The Scots were aware of young Charles' distrust
Of their League and Covenant. But needs must…

The King agreed, on his most "solemn oath"
And before God ("searcher of hearts"), the oaf,
To full "Presbyterial government",
As approved by the Kirk. Royal assent
(Believe it or not) he would also give
For the imposition (yes, as I live)
Of Presbyterianism throughout
His other "dominions". Have no doubt,
This was a stitch-up, a regular rout.

The final insult to this injury
Lay in his agreement (given for free)
To observe, within his own family,
Presbyterian practice. Charles, you see,
Cared not a fig for episcopacy.

Or did he? Well, that's the promise he gave.
His grandfather, James? He turned in his grave.
Remember his pledge? "No Bishop, no King."
His grandson's words had a cynical ring.

Charles the Second and the Restoration

King Charles had no intention, however,
Of keeping his word. Cynical? Clever?
Opportunistic? Cunning? Whatever…
Suffice it to say, the King would never
(I repeat, never) have sworn what he swore
Had he any idea what now lay in store.

He sailed for Scotland in 1650,
In mid-summer. The Scots he found thrifty –
That's putting it mildly. They were plain mean,
In Charles' opinion (best to come clean).
Long sermons became his staple diet,
Once four in a row (you care to try it?).
He was made to repent his father's ills.
Then came Dunbar, that most bitter of pills.
Oliver Cromwell, against all the odds,
Gave rout to the Scots. The triumph was God's,
So claimed the victor, who offered up thanks.
The Scots' high command, though, had purged their ranks
Of some of their bravest veterans, then
(God help us) replaced them with lesser men –
Religious fellows, ministers' sons,
With no taste for battle, bloodshed or guns.
As strategies go, distinctly unwise:
Defeat was assured, to no one's surprise.

Charles might well be forgiven a wry smile.
An effective prisoner all the while,
The wholesale slaughter of his Scottish 'foes'
Was hardly, to Charles, the worst of his woes.
He was still stuck in Scotland, however.
He'd little option but to persever,
As best he could, in his royal campaign –
And you know what they say: no pain, no gain.

1651 saw some improvement
In the King's depressing predicament.

Rhyming History

New Year's Day witnessed his coronation.
After a day of humiliation,
In late December, in which the nation
Took cognisance of the sins of the King
And his Stuart forebears (if anything,
Worse than a jagged dagger to his heart),
Charles' crowning at Scone signalled a new start.
The Scots, eager to see him play his part,
Now buttered him up (this I call smarmy),
Put him in sole command of the Army,
And prepared for its ready deployment
South of the border. Charles, in employment
For once in his life, was a man new born.

His prospects, alas, were sadly forlorn.
As his Army marched south in late summer,
Charles was greeted not as a newcomer,
Or a liberator, but rather, at best,
As an awkward, unbidden, unwelcome guest.
A nightmare. Charles had been led to expect
A surge of royalist support. Respect,
Though, for the King had been ebbing away,
Among his allies, ever since the day,
That dread day, that he'd signed the Covenant.
His conduct, they felt, was not consonant
With their old, Anglican aspirations,
Now under threat. Such considerations
Were deadly. Charles need not have been surprised.
His supporters were so demoralised,
Fretful, fearful, depressed, disorganised
(Or simply worn out) that they stayed indoors –
Sick to the stomach of more civil wars.

Worcester

Twenty-four days on the march took their toll.
With Cromwell (popularly known as Noll)
In hottest pursuit (he was on a roll),

Charles the Second and the Restoration

The Scots' Army (for that's how folk saw it:
Though led by Charles, they couldn't ignore it)
Was famished, exhausted, cold and footsore.
It fetched up in Worcester. The final straw
Was that Cromwell's troops were already there!
He'd marched them down with his usual flair.
His forces, it seemed, were everywhere.

Charles nonetheless occupied the city.
Worcester's small, narrow streets (more's the pity)
Afforded the King what Oliver lacked –
A firm, defensive base. As he attacked,
He held the advantage, and that's a fact.

Rhyming History

What he was short of (I'll say this with tact)
Were men. It's true. For when all's said and done,
The Scots were outnumbered by two to one.

Worcester, however, was most keenly fought –
A tighter battle than many first thought.
"As stiff a contest as ever I saw,"
Volunteered Noll – and he knew about war.
The King fought with valour, all were agreed,
Yet no one believed he'd ever succeed.
Five hours they battled. Conjecture was right:
2,000 poor Scots perished, and by twilight
On the 3rd of September (which, by the way,
Was the date of Dunbar, a year to the day)
The royalist remnants just melted away –
The brave King among them. I do have to say
That the field resembled the end of a play,
With the corpses piled high in the cobbled streets –
Most mournful of scenes; most horrid of defeats.

On the run

So where to now? Were his cause to survive,
Charles must escape. To be taken alive,
A prisoner King: a cipher, a pawn
In enemy hands… He'd never been born
A Prince, a Stuart, to suffer such fate.
He must take to flight. It wasn't too late.
As night closed in, by the northernmost gate
He slipped out of Worcester. And so began
His astonishing journey. Charles, the man,
Proved himself dogged, determined and bold,
Resourceful and honest… So Pepys was told
(By the King himself!), as Samuel reveals
In his famous *Diary*. For Pepys, one feels,
Honoured his dread sovereign, as well he might.
His *Diary*, at times, is far from polite;

Charles the Second and the Restoration

But for Charles he'd nothing but admiration
And here, one senses, he spoke for the nation.

The fugitive headed he knew not where,
Yet contrived to vanish into thin air.
Intrepid, and a stranger to despair,
The King kept his wits, all too well aware
That he was fighting for his very life.
Lost in a land where treachery was rife,
One thousand pounds was the price on his head –
A stupendous sum, it has to be said.
The courage of folk that the King did meet,
Who offered him comfort, and food to eat,
Was wondrous to witness. With bleeding feet,
Clothes torn and face blackened (a sorry sight),
He and his retinue rode through the night –
Viz. Buckingham and the Earl of Derby.

The plucky Earl it was, apparently,
Who saved Charles' bacon with the suggestion
They head in a northerly direction.
He knew the rough lay-out of the terrain
From a former, unsuccessful campaign.
The Giffords, a Catholic family,
Were glad to give him shelter. They, you see,
Recognised the value of trusty friends
In troubled times. Perhaps to make amends,
The good King, after his Restoration,
Sought to remedy the situation
By promising Catholics liberty
And freedom of conscience. His loyalty
And sense of fairness were legendary.
Reform, however, there wasn't to be.
Parliament dug in its heels. Who are we
To demur? Still, a missed opportunity.

I digress. Charles split off from Buckingham.
The Penderel brothers (all five of them)

Rhyming History

Became his mainstay for a week or two.
Charles disguised himself (a smart thing to do)
As a country bumpkin (well, wouldn't you?).
Safety he sought in various priest-holes.
A servant was one of his many 'roles',
Riding with his 'lady' to Bristol, there
To seek a ship. He found none anywhere –
Not of a royalist colour, at least.
Father Huddlestone, a Catholic priest,
Who crops up later in this strange story,
Shielded the King from the sound and fury
Of the chase. Everywhere: loyalty,
Deference and respect for royalty.
Charles met with narrow escapes, near misses,
Close shaves… and not a few stolen kisses.
The King was ever true to form, you see –
Who cared if this was an emergency?

The stuff of legend. Six weeks on the run.
In retrospect, it all sounds rather fun.

An oak tree featured. No doubt about that.
Some say it's a myth, but I'll eat my hat
If the tale isn't true. Major Careless
(You couldn't make it up), in some distress,
Had taken refuge near Boscobel Wood.
He tipped off Charles, as a good subject should –
He was on the run, what else could he do? –
That enemy soldiers (more than a few)
Were combing the country. Next on the list
Was the Penderels' house. You get the gist.
Careless and Charles, not a moment too soon,
Fled to the wood where, the whole afternoon,
They hid in a tree – no word of a joke.
The soldiers wandered from oak to oak,
Beating the undergrowth, rooting around,
But keeping their noses close to the ground.

Charles the Second and the Restoration

The King, however, had fallen asleep
On Careless's arm. His breathing was deep;
He'd had cheese for his lunch and beer to drink.
He was sure to snore and (what do you think?)
The Major's arm had gone totally numb,
His shoulder was sore – and so was his bum.

Should he wake the King and should Charles cry out,
They could wave goodbye, no shadow of doubt,
To liberty and life. Oh, happy day!
Charles woke with a start, but I'm glad to say
Without so much as a snore or a snort –
Or he and Careless had surely been caught.

Rhyming History

England celebrated Oak Apple Day –
The King's birthday, the 29th of May –
For years as an annual holiday.
It's now considered a trifle *passé*,
Save by the Stuart Society. Hey,
Let 'em alone to make merry, I say.

After forty fraught and dangerous days,
The King, whose exploits would ever amaze,
Found a ship prepared to take him to France.
Her captain recognised Charles at a glance
And weighed up the odds. He would take the risk.
The wind was fresh and the passage was brisk.
The King set foot, with a sigh of relief,
On the soil of France. It's my belief
That his joy, at best, was mingled with grief.
Ahead of him lay (he knew it, you see)
Long years, if not decades, of poverty –
Dependent (he loathed it) on charity.
He was right, for that's what they proved to be.

A footnote. Derby was executed
The very day Charles set sail: saluted
By Royalists; all but forgotten
By history. Appalling. Rotten.

The Court in exile

Autumn 1651. Nine years it took –
An immensely long time in anyone's book –
Before Charles the Second came into his own,
Restored, as was proper and right, to his throne.
The tedious months up to that happy time
Were an agony. The King was in his prime,
And suffered the terrible ignominy
Of living in a state of near beggary.
His pathetic 'Court' was sadly depleted.
Poor Hyde professed himself all but defeated

Charles the Second and the Restoration

By the lack of funds. In the harsh French winter
They'd no wood for fires – no, not a splinter!

This, of course, makes nonsense of the rumours (spread
By the King's enemies, it has to be said)
Of Charles' recklessness, nay, his extravagance.
True, to keep his pecker up, he liked to dance
And few begrudged him this (though Hyde looked askance).
The King craved recreation, and this was France,
After all. As was his wont, he took his chance,
Too, with the ladies. I've read (I forget where)
That his 'proclivities' drove Hyde to despair:
In excess of fifteen mistresses, we're told,
In as many months! But the winters were cold
And the King hot-blooded. Who was Hyde to scold?

In 1653 Cromwell's Commonwealth
Formed an alliance with France. Not for his health
Did Charles quit the country. He was thrown out.
He'd outstayed his welcome, no word of a doubt.

The French paid him a pension (every cloud…)
In their bid to be rid of him. Charles, unbowed,
Professed himself hurt, if not a little peeved.
In his heart, of course, he was mighty relieved.
Holland wouldn't have him. It's complicated:
Content at first, they later hesitated.
So he struck out with his *entourage* for Spa,
Just north of Luxemburg and not all that far
From the Spanish Netherlands; then to Cologne,
Via Aachen. Charles didn't travel alone.
He had Princess Mary with him, his sister.
The Dutch hadn't found it hard to resist her:
Cool and aloof, when the Prince of Orange died
(Her husband, William), Mary was denied
A widow's deference. She was cast adrift,
Distrusted by the Dutch. They gave her short shrift.

Rhyming History

She clung to her brother, siblings in exile.
The French, the Dutch and the English all the while
Forged their poisonous alliances. Who cared
For the ousted Stuarts? I should have despaired.
But the King? Never. News from England was grim.
Penruddock's revolt had failed. Prospects were dim.
For Charles, though? Pessimism wasn't for him –
Simply not his style. In 1655
His almost exhausted hopes were kept alive
By the propect of war (the benefits plain)
Between Oliver Cromwell's England and Spain.
Should Charles join the hostilities on Spain's side,
Then… Bob's your uncle! It might just turn the tide.
Was this likely? It didn't appeal to Hyde.
Still, you've heard of Castles in Spain. You decide.

Oliver had upset the Spanish somewhat
By capturing Jamaica, an action not
(I repeat, not) entirely to their liking –
Anathema, indeed, to their scornful King.
His pride sorely wounded, the following spring
He declared war. Now, if there's any one thing
That a Spaniard values above his pride,
I have yet to unearth it. Charles wrote to Hyde
In earnest and eager terms. An alliance
With Spain was surely now on the cards. Finance,
To no one's surprise, played a crucial part
In negotiations. Charles (a good start)
Would receive (hurrah!) a handsome allowance.

Handsome? Ha! To his chagrin and annoyance,
Little (if any, indeed) came to be paid.
Well, so be it. More undertakings were made,
Including support from Spain for Charles' campaign
(If you can call his efforts that) to regain
His throne. In return for this promise, Charles pledged –
The details are hazy, but so it's alleged –

To suspend England's long-standing penal laws
Against Catholics. Though worthy of applause,
This at very best was an aspiration,
Given England's prejudice, as a nation,
Against the Church of Rome. All this we shall see.

The 'treaty', quite frankly, was mere fantasy
And came in the end to nothing. Charles agreed,
Moreover, to order, with all decent speed,
Those soldiers that he had fighting for France
To switch instead to Spain – his brothers (fat chance!)
Among them. James, Duke of York, was furious.
His war record in France had been glorious,
Serving his young cousin, Louis. In a huff,
He flounced off to Holland. Enough was enough.
Mary, Charles' sister, was miserable too.
Spain was her enemy, everyone knew,
As Princess of Orange – but what could she do?

Charles moved to the Spanish Netherlands, meanwhile,
To be nearer the action. Here his exile
(Sad, empty years) continued unabated.
Far from the breakthrough he'd anticipated,
The Spanish treaty proved a dud. James did fight,
Eventually (be assured this is right –
It's more than a little complex), on Spain's side
Against France, and certainly no one denied
His courage. But the Spanish were defeated
At the Battle of the Dunes – bloody, heated
And hard-fought. This was in 1658.
Charles had advanced not a jot. Was it too late?

The death of Cromwell

The King was playing tennis (ready to serve)
When the glad tidings reached him. He held his nerve
And finished the set (I've embroidered a bit):
Oliver Cromwell was dead – some sort of fit,

Rhyming History

According to first reports. Just imagine!
The rejoicing! It's said they could hear the din
In Antwerp, some fifteen miles distant or more.

Sadly, the celebrations were premature.
The King was set to wait some twenty months before
His blessed Restoration. An open door?
Hardly. This came to many as a surprise.
With the tyrant dead, men could only surmise
That the whole Protectorate would have to go,
Lock, stock and rotten barrel. Sadly, not so.
"So great a calm we are in," wrote John Thurloe,
"There is not a dog that wags his tongue." Slow, slow
Was the long progress towards Restoration.

Was it mere apathy that gripped the nation?
All good folk were poised, surely, with bated breath
For their sovereign's homecoming. Cromwell's death,
Unexpected as it was (at fifty-nine),
Left a dangerous void. Who was next in line?

Charles the Second and the Restoration

Easy to answer! He'd named Richard, his son,
As his successor. To the surprise of none,
Dick failed to measure up to his mighty pa –
But nominated he was, so there we are.
Foreign governments were loth, to say the least,
To throw in their lot with Charles. Expected feast,
Then, gave way to famine. There was no great taste
For the Stuarts, and far from indecent haste
To offer backing for Charles; no appetite
For renewed conflict; no stomach for a fight.

Poor Tumbledown Dick's fall the following year
Caused few subjects to shed more than the odd tear,
Yet failed to fuel new enthusiasm
For the royalist cause. There was a chasm,
Still, in the popular imagination
Between the prosperity of the nation
And the prospect of a restored monarchy.
The downtrodden populace, it seems to me,
Had been brainwashed (a desperate policy),
Stunned into a state of leaden apathy
And left wary and fretful. That's tyranny!

An attempted *coup*, designed to stop the rot,
Led by one Sir George Booth, failed. Like it or not,
Despite Dick's exit, Charles couldn't get a grip.
What must have really given him the pip
Were the differences between Charles Fleetwood,
John Desborough and John Lambert. These rows should,
Were there any justice, have had folk flocking
To his flag. Yet Fortune failed to come knocking.
Nobody had a clue! People were appalled
When the old Rump Parliament was recalled.

The Army was rumbling with discontent,
At odds ('twas ever thus) with Parliament.
Republic, Commonwealth (call it what you will),
The Protectorate, had run its course. Yet still,

Rhyming History

Can you believe, on the brink of anarchy,
They failed to call for the King. How could this be?
Well, for one thing, Charles had a bad press, you see.
Thurloe's spies (he'd been Oliver's eyes and ears)
Had painted a grim portrait, from what one hears:
Dissolute, idle, indulgent, immoral,
Catholic, 'absolute' and quick to quarrel.

Changing fortunes

When the tide did turn, it turned suddenly.
One thing Monck abhorred and that was anarchy.
The General was a trooper through and through,
A loyal servant to the state. Monck knew
The hour was his. No regicide he,
George craved the order and stability
Of sound government – and he was the key.
He proved himself worthy to bend the knee
To the King's sovereign authority.

Monck was a man of some few words, cool,
Discreet, unflappable – nobody's fool.
He'd served with distinction (at forty-four)
As an Admiral in the first Dutch War.
Earlier still, on the field at Dunbar,
He won his spurs. He was sure to go far.
Governor of Scotland (by appointment
Of Cromwell) Monck proved no disappointment.
Taciturn, honest, brave and respected,
On old Noll's death he quickly accepted
Richard's authority – no question.
Disorder caused him indigestion.

When poor Dick fell, George supported the Rump,
But Fleetwood and Lambert gave him the hump.
Should their fractious conduct (so opined Monck)
Continue unchecked, then England was sunk.

Charles the Second and the Restoration

They expelled the Rump, recalled it again,
Then Fleetwood resigned (it's hard to explain:
He lost his nerve I can only suppose),
Leaving Lambert in charge, though how (God knows)
This jumped-up, inadequate popinjay
Expected to rule I really can't say.

Breaking the sworn habit of a lifetime,
General George (England's only lifeline)
Marched south to seize the initiative.
Lambert, in turn (this I cannot forgive),
Headed north to confront him. As I live,
His fragile force simply melted away.
Fairfax came out of the woodwork (hooray!)
In support of our George. Good show, I say –
A stout chap, Sir Thomas. Oh, by the way,
The King, Charles the Second, one understands,
A bystander still in the Netherlands,
Waited and watched, nothing to do with it.
As events unfolded, though, bit by bit,
He welcomed developments (jolly good news)
As should you, dear reader, whatever your views.

Nobody's certain just how sure Monck was
Of his basic objective. That's because,
Historians all are agreed, his heart
He rarely wore on his sleeve. George's part,
Nonetheless, in the King's Restoration
Was pivotal. It behoves the nation,
Even today, to be duly grateful.
To argue otherwise? Truly hateful.

Poor England was sick. John Evelyn wrote –
And this is *verbatim*, kindly take note:
"We have no government in the nation,
"All in confusion… " Some indication,
I should hazard, of a tottering state,
Lawless and desperate. "No magistrate,"

John complained, "either owned or pretended",
The law, it appears, all but suspended.
"God Almighty" (Evelyn was to plead)
"Have mercy on and settle us… " His need,
England's too, was for peace and good order,
And George Monck's record north of the border
Gave hope to men such as Evelyn, who
Were rooting for Charles, but hadn't a clue
Just how they could help or what they should do.

Monck bowled up in the nick of time (no doubt),
Just as other options were running out.
Folk were frantic for a change of *régime*
And Charles was riding high in their esteem.
First and foremost, the King was no Catholic –
Contrary rumours made them heartily sick.
Charles was well fit for government, thanks to Hyde.
The timing was perfect, it can't be denied.
People were ready to welcome their King.
Nothing suited England better, nothing.

Monck's manoeuvres

Monck made a serious error at first
By siding with the Rump. Men feared the worst.
He managed, which surprises me rather,
To whip up London into a lather.
He "exceedingly exasperated
"The City" – Evelyn's words. Berated,
And in danger of losing their favour,
Monck offered the citizens some flavour
Of his 'cool' (and his flexibility)
By heeding the demands of the City.
George guaranteed, under his protection,
The return (no need for fresh election)
Of those members purged by Colonel Pride
From the Long Parliament. Though they tried,
Die-hards failed to stem the popular tide.

Charles the Second and the Restoration

The Rump was thus effectively killed off,
Swamped by the 'secluded' members. Don't scoff,
But rumps of beef were roasted, publicly,
In the streets of London – a "jubilee,"
Wrote Evelyn, reporting it with glee.

The Long Parliament, twenty years old,
Voted with relish (at least, so we're told)
To dissolve itself. This move paved the way
For 'free' elections. Monck, I have to say,
Played a blinder. He was aware, of course,
That Royalists would be returned in force
To the new assembly. George was clever.
He never at this stage (repeat, never)

Rhyming History

Announced his support for the King. Canny
And cautious, he'd have sold his own granny
Before openly declaring his hand.

Not that Monck was idle, you understand.
Far from it. Putting nothing in writing –
This, you'll agree, is getting exciting –
He replied to a letter from the King,
By secret messenger. There was one thing,
He advised, that Charles could usefully do:
Move away from Brussels. Well, wouldn't you?
To stay in the Spanish Netherlands? Bad.
Remain in a Catholic country? Mad.
On Hyde's advice, the best place to be had
In a hurry was Breda, to the north,
In Holland. The Court duly sallied forth,
Gaining supporters (of course!) by the day.
Good-natured Charles couldn't turn them away,
Though toadies and turncoats, I do have to say.

Charles prepares the ground

From Breda the King sent to Parliament
His respects. A friendly message he sent,
Flattering its members. England had need
Of both Kings and Parliaments, Charles agreed.
A far more significant document –
First, halting steps towards a settlement –
Was the Declaration of Breda. Hyde,
The King's one counsellor, mentor and guide
Through thick and thin (and now Lord Chancellor),
Was the document's true progenitor
And should take due credit, the best of men.
It was pitch-perfect: ten out of ten;
Fit for purpose: all things to all men!

Now, mark the terms of the Declaration.
Charles promised (surely an aspiration?)

Charles the Second and the Restoration

"Liberty", if Parliament approved,
"To tender consciences". Sadly, unmoved,
Members 'declined' when it came to the crunch.

Did the King suspect this? Well, it's my hunch
(Given the outcome) Hyde certainly did.
The Commons gave up the chance to be rid
Of the stench of religious bigotry.
They refused the first fence! This we shall see.
They blew it, their best opportunity –
The fools, the fools… Less contentious, far less,
Was the King's full promise of forgiveness
("Grace and favour") to all his enemies.
Quick to forget and determined to please,
Only foul regicides he excepted.
This generous pardon, as expected,
Healed many a festering wound at a stroke.
Charles, after all, was a sensible bloke.

Parliament, too, was offered the task
Of restoring estates. This, since you ask,
Was a pretty sore point. 'Sequestration',
As it was called, divided the nation.
Royalists had been obliged to sell land
To pay fines. Some others, more underhand,
Had hung onto theirs and found other ways
Of discharging their dues. In those dark days,
Justice (to grace it with the name) was rough.
Church and Crown lands were restored. Fair enough.
But other folk suffered grievously.
Stuffed! Landless gentry! Quite literally!

Before we move on, one last, vital part
Of the King's pledge (which Monck took in good heart)
Was the promise to honour Army pay.
This issue seemed never to go away.
Arrears were a constant bugbear, I'd say,
And Charles thought it time to call it a day.

Rhyming History

An invitation

Events began to move at quite a lick.
The Declaration seemed to do the trick.
The House of Commons, clearly excited,
Rose to the occasion and 'invited'
(Odd word, though strangely apt) the exiled King
Home to his kingdom, his for the taking!

The invitation, proffered on May Day,
Was the more remarkable, I should say,
For placing not one single condition
On Charles' return. The unique position
Of Parliament (central, you might think)
Was left a blank. The Commons' powers? Blink,
And you missed them. Astonishing, but true –
As if, after ten long years, people knew
That the Republic, rotten through and through,
Was dead in the water. Its time was up.
Resentment was rife. They'd been sold a pup.

Nothing could be worse, men agreed, nothing,
Than Cromwell and his cronies. Anything
Were better. Besides, you could trust a King!

Hear something? That'll be Francis Pym,
Turning in his grave. Remember him?
Remember Charles the First, indeed,
Whose follies made poor England bleed –
All but forgotten in the rush
To restore his son? At first blush,
It's all too easy to overlook
Popular prejudice. In my book,
However mean, corrupt or rotten
A King may be, he's soon forgotten.
Ditto a tyrant, like Cromwell.
So, what of this Charles? Time will tell.

Charles the Second and the Restoration

Forgive me, but what I'm trying to say,
Albeit in quite a roundabout way,
Is that once old England made up her mind
To ask Charles back, it seemed rather unkind
To impose constraints – if not downright rude.
The King, I'm delighted to say, was shrewd.
He'd the strength to back down when times were bad,
So held onto his crown – unlike his dad.

For indeed there were times, more than a few,
When the only reliable thing to do
Was to bow to the will of Parliament.
For the Commons controlled the purse strings. This meant
That the King, sad to say, was ever constrained
By the realities of finance. Charles reigned,
But did he rule? He rarely put a foot wrong,
In my view (but then, I'm a fan). When on song,
He was flexible, fair, pragmatic and strong.
Yet they made it all up as they went along,
He and the Commons (with the odd *contretemps*).
This we'll see. The Declaration, after all,
Left much to Parliament, as you'll recall.
When the Commons, for instance, set out its stall
In matters religious, Charles was appalled.
The bigotry! The 'Clarendon Code' (so-called),
Regressive and wrong, was a clear case in point.
King and the Commons were soon out of joint.

Such ructions, however, lay ahead. For now,
It was fun, feasting and festival, and how!

Charles was presented with fifty thousand pounds,
Sent over from England. The figure astounds.
His state of euphoria (this I have read)
Was such that he spread (if I've not been misled)
This abundance of wealth all over his bed.
"Brother James! Sister Mary!" he cried with glee,
His fingers alive with the coins. "Come and see!" –

A spectacle of innocent ecstasy,
Acceptable (well, just) it occurs to me,
When set against the anguish and agony
Of those long years of begging and penury,
Leavened only by pity and charity.

Home at last

The King sailed home in the good ship *Naseby* –
Sorry, it was rechristened, hastily,
The *Royal Charles* (the former name, you see,
Rather less than appropriate). At sea,
Charles appeared to be in his element.
Between The Hague and Dover, resentment –
If indeed he had ever felt any –
Gave way to stories (now two a penny)
Of his escape from Worcester (that oak tree),

Charles the Second and the Restoration

The Penderel brothers (their loyalty),
His time in Scotland (the hostility),
His exile in Holland (then Germany),
His wanderings through Europe… These, clearly,
Reminded Charles of the fragility
Of his estate. He was keen to the strain.
Once home, he never left England again.

General Monck met the King at Dover.
A token that Charles' exile was over
Was the presentation of his sheathed sword
(Monck's, that is). A further bull's-eye was scored
When Dover's Mayor presented the King
With a copy of the Bible. Nothing,
Charles assured him (how he kept a straight face),
Would he treasure above this. A disgrace,
But never mind. Kings have to learn to lie.
All things to all men they must be, that's why.

Charles' royal progress stretched over four days.
The splendour! The pomp! The towns were ablaze!
From Dover and thence to Canterbury,
Then Rochester, his popularity
Was palpable, patent and plain to see.
At Blackheath he encountered his Army,
'Introduced' by Monck. Where did power lie?
Good question. It were hard to deny
That George was firmly in the driving seat.
Or was he? Best to keep the old man sweet,
Butter him up, let matters take their course,
And never, ever, try to rule by force.

A triumphant return

So the King entered London. His birthday,
By happy chance, fell on that favoured day:
Thirty years old – the 29th of May.

Rhyming History

Charles took full advantage, as was his way,
Of this fitting coincidence. I'd say
(Were I asked) it was timed to perfection.
Stage-managed? Have you any objection?
If people are starved of spectacle, fine –
Let 'em have it! The fountains flowed with wine.
The Venetian Ambassador (stout chap)
Offered a regular supply, on tap.
Bottoms up, Venice! It took seven hours
For the royal procession to pass. Towers,
Walls, balconies – all were bedecked with flowers;
The streets hung with banners and tapestries;
Companies all in their finest liveries,
With the Mayor and Aldermen, if you please,
In chains of gold; windows "well-set" with ladies;
Heralds, footmen and lackeys; noble lords, clad
In rich cloth of silver and velvet. Not bad,
I'd say, for a people so lately deprived
Of colour and show. They seem to have survived!

You think I'm embroidering? Take a look
(It's well worth it) at John Evelyn's book,
His *Diary*. The detail, it's all there.
An acute eye-witness, writing with flair,
His account is astonishing. The din,
Above all, as described by Evelyn,
Is what, three and a half centuries on,
Endures. The actors are long dead and gone,
But hear the hubbub! Folk are still "shouting
"With unexpressable joy… bells ringing,
"Ladies, trumpets, music... " with crowds "flocking
"The streets… " And in the midst of this, one man,
Silent, reflecting how it all began.

"I stood in the Strand," John Evelyn writes,
"And beheld it" (his report still excites)
"And blessed God." A miracle, plain to see:
The King restored, "by the very army

"Which rebelled against him". It was, truly,
"The Lord's doing". Who are we to disagree?
It was, indeed, "past all human policy".

The end of a tiring day

The Commons' Speaker, I have to confess,
Exhausted the King with his long address.
Seven hours' travel! Charles was worn out,
Yet was forced to respond (he had no doubt)
To this boring, tedious oration.
Charles in his wisdom used the occasion
To flatter the Commons. He'd have them know,
Whatever they wanted he'd have it so.

Utter humbug, of course. He spent the night –
Having opted out, if I've got this right,
Of a Thanksgiving Service (far too tired) –
In the arms of his mistress, the admired,
The adored, Barbara Palmer. Vicious
She was, according to some. Delicious,
In Pepys' humble view (he was curious,
Nay, smitten). Barbara was notorious,
A fabled beauty with "wistful blue eyes"
(Lord Clarendon's phrase). It's no great surprise,
Given her figure and rich auburn hair,
That she held the King (this isn't unfair)
A slave to her charms for full seven years.

A mistress of tantrums, temper and tears,
Charles (bless his heart) could deny her nothing.
She bore him five children (that's quite something),
All openly acknowledged. Pensioned off
As her bloom of youth faded, Babs (don't scoff),
Countess of Castlemaine, and Duchess now
Of Cleveland, made a small fortune, and how!
Her sexual adventures continued –
Forgive me, I know this is rather rude –

Rhyming History

As mistress to the popular playwright,
William Wycherley, and (hold on tight)
The rope-dancer, Jacob Hall. Yes, that's right –
An agile acrobat, from the circus!

The King's character

Sorry, this has been quite an *excursus*.
Its significance, though, it seems to me,
Is it sets Charles' character to a T.
Many mistake his liberality
For licence, lust and immorality;
His openness and generosity
For recklessness and prodigality.
True, though, when it came to matrimony,
The King came a cropper – very nearly.

Queen Catherine professed quite sincerely,
Right from the start, that she loved Charles dearly.
She refused to accept, though (nor would you),
His resident mistress. What a to-do!
Babs wasn't ready to call it a day.
Charles was appalled, but too weak to give way.
Poor Catherine swooned, she stormed and she screamed,
Then suddenly settled. Who could have dreamed
That this fragile, sweet and sensitive soul
Would have shown such spirit? Now, on the whole,
It's Charles that I blame, capricious and vain.
He had his Queen, yet kept his Castlemaine!

I digress. Catherine is two years hence.
But with Babs about, I thought it made sense
To give you a flavour (well, just a taste)
Of future upheavals. Now on, with haste…

The Declaration of Breda in practice

The restored King had the intelligence
To seek to heal wounds. Revenge was nonsense.
"Grace and favour", as I'm sure you'll recall,
Was central to the Declaration. All,
However, could not be pardoned. The King,
His father, had been murdered and nothing
Could disguise that awful fact. Regicides
Must answer and if this meant taking sides,
So be it. The 'Convention' Parliament
(Monck's, that is), legitimate to the extent
That its unique but dodgy authority
Could only be confirmed retrospectively
(It lacked the royal writ originally),
Passed, thank heavens, the Act of Indemnity
And Oblivion. This pardoned, sweepingly,
All but the worst of the regicides, fifty
At most – the ones who'd been most closely involved
In the vile and bloody deed. So, problem solved.

Rhyming History

Or was it? Well, feelings did run pretty deep,
If truth be told. It's enough to make you weep,
But on the anniversary, to the day,
Of the King's foul murder (sick, I have to say)
They dug up Cromwell's body and (oh, brother!)
The corpse of his poor, unfortunate mother.
They disinterred, too, the remains of Pym, Blake,
Ireton and Bradshaw. Why, for pity's sake,
This was considered at all appropriate
Beats me. About as ghoulish as you can get,
But (can you believe?) I haven't finished yet.

The corpses of Cromwell and his son-in-law,
Ireton, and the long-suffering Bradshaw
Were dragged through the streets (much merriment, no doubt)
And publicly hanged at Tyburn. So, watch out,
I'm warning you, if you've been contemplating
The execution of an anointed King.
Our friend, John Evelyn, witnessed the event
And thanked God for his "inscrutable judgement".

Whether Charles approved of this monstrous deed,
I doubt. He simply didn't feel the need.
A handful of regicides, though, were tried,
Thomas Harrison among those who died.
A Major-General, and right-hand man
To Cromwell, Harrison was no great fan
Of the King. He didn't believe in fudge.
When Charles came to trial, he was a judge.
He signed the death warrant. A regicide
To his very bones, it were suicide
To stay put after the new King's return.
But Thomas Harrison showed no concern
For his own safety. He made no attempt
To flee, bearing nothing but low contempt
For cowards. Nay, why should he be exempt
From the rough justice of retribution?

He said of the late King's execution
It "was not a thing done in a corner".
He laid no claim to being a mourner.
Charles was a tyrant. He deserved to die.
Now his own time had come and that was why,
According to reports, he looked cheerful
(Pepys' odd epithet) and far from fearful.
Hung, drawn and quartered (for that was the style),
His face in death wore the hint of a smile.
His heart was held out to the crowd. What joy!
They loved a good death by hanging. Oh, boy!

But Charles was disgusted. He wrote to Hyde:
"I am weary of hangings." You decide,
Was he foolish or just? It seems to me
That he kept his head. You may not agree.

New appointments

In his choice of ministers the King, too,
Was seen to be even-handed. It's true
That this ruffled feathers (more than a few).
Please ask yourselves, though, what else could he do?
Edward Hyde, the mainstay of his exile,
Was, of his allies, the highest profile.
Lord Chancellor he became, his reward
For loyalty of service. Charles got bored,
Eventually, with Hyde's priggishness,
His petty ways and his niggardliness,
And fired him, the first Earl of Clarendon –
As Hyde became in 1661.
A sorry case. He'd already begun
His great *History of the Rebellion*
In exile. Now banished for a second time,
He finished his *magnum opus*. Past his prime?
You have got to be joking. It's quite sublime.

45

Rhyming History

Now, where was I? The King's ministers, yes.
A mixed bag. General George Monck, no less,
Became Lord Lieutenant of Ireland (bless!) –
Out of harm's way. Rather greater distress
Was caused when one of the King's former foes,
Anthony Ashley Cooper (who, God knows,
Later became a right royal wrecker),
Was made Chancellor of the Exchequer.
Ashley Cooper had joined Charles in exile,
But jumped ship. Constancy wasn't his style.
He sailed back to England and, if you please,
At a time when the King was on his knees,
Joined the republican Council of State.
Never known to blush or hesitate,
Cooper was one of the delegation
That welcomed the King, at Restoration,
Back to his own country. An arrant knave!
What nerve! What sauce! What a way to behave!

Charles the Second and the Restoration

Charles, however, had the sense and good grace
To keep him on side and let him save face.
Ashley wasn't the sole 'republican'
To take up office when Charles' reign began.
Ministers were appointed, to a man,
With an eye to the future, not the past.
The King's new government was built to last.

Even the judges who had served Cromwell
Were confirmed in their appointments. Expel
The justices? Charles knew only too well
What disruption and chaos that would cause.
This showed some courage and merits applause.

The Army was accommodated too.
Charles grasped the nettle. Arrears of pay due
Were paid – an expensive operation,
But needful for the health of the nation.
The New Model Army was disbanded.
Charles might well have felt a little stranded
When the new 'Cavalier' Parliament
Refused to accept (nay, was adamant)
That a King was in need of an Army,
Which to me seems more than a tad barmy.
Charles took it all in his stride. Very wise,
But this must have come as quite a surprise.

Yet there was scarcely a voice of protest
Raised (fairly striking, it must be confessed)
Against his personal, absolute right
To appoint his ministers. Hold on tight.
This was a key issue at stake, by God,
In the late Rebellion. Now, on the nod,
It was wholly accepted. All very odd.

A more subversive and bitter impact
Was caused by the controversial Act

Rhyming History

Of Indemnity (ambiguous word)
And Oblivion. It was too absurd,
Felt some, that the King's former enemies
Should suffer far less than they, if you please,
Who'd been constant to Charles through thick and thin.
Whatever they did they just couldn't win.

Indemnity for his foes, said the wits;
Mere oblivion for his friends. The pits!

The Church

So to religion, never easy –
Indeed, the whole topic makes me queasy.
But here goes. Charles in his Declaration
Spoke (no word of an exaggeration)
Of his intention to grant "liberty
"To tender consciences". He was, you see,
A born healer, nay, a visionary.
Sorry if that's overstating the case –
He'd an open heart and that's no disgrace.
No one was more optimistic than he.

Sadly, however, it wasn't to be.
All began well enough. A conference
Was convened (and this made absolute sense)
At Clarendon's lodgings, Worcester House,
To discuss Church matters. Charles had the nous
To try to 'nail' religion early.
Anglicans, he understood, were surly –
As you'd expect, the way they'd been treated
By Cromwell and Co. Debate was heated.
Yet the King strove hard for a settlement,
Limiting (this occasioned resentment)
The powers of bishops – even, indeed,
Offering bishoprics, with all due speed,
To moderate Presbyterians. Well,
This was highly unlikely, truth to tell,

Charles the Second and the Restoration

To cut any ice with Parliament.
This clumsy attempt at a settlement
Was destined, alas, to fall on deaf ears.

The following year there were further tears.
The new Parliament, as expected –
The Cavalier, duly elected –
Was of a stronger Anglican flavour
Than the Convention. Its behaviour
Was intolerant, bigoted, unjust
And backward. I have to say this, I must.
Its wicked influence was divisive
And malign; the damage done, decisive.

Fine, but what did it actually do,
This Cavalier Parliament? In my view,
For what it's worth, nothing constructive at all.
Reactionary, and in for the long haul,
Its members were clearly resolved, to a man,
To crush non-conformity and so began
A programme of measures to outlaw dissent
Which even his Majesty couldn't prevent.

First, bishops were restored to the House of Lords –
No big deal, you'll agree. What struck deeper chords
Was that all members (no exceptions, please note)
Were obliged (this by an overwhelming vote)
To take the sacrament according, of course,
To the Church of England. I ask you, what sauce!

A revised Prayer Book was then accepted
By Parliament and forced (as expected)
On the country at large – or on those, at least,
Who sought public office. An Anglican feast!
The wheel had turned full circle. Dissenters: out!
Quakers, Presbyterians, Baptists: a rout!
This campaign was underpinned, without a doubt,
By a hatred of Catholics. Papists, watch out!

Rhyming History

A whole raft of statutes (the Clarendon Code)
Was swiftly enacted, which sought to erode
The rights of non-conformists – a rocky road
For those who sought to hold true, as was their right,
To their godly beliefs. Tolerance: good night.

The Corporation Act (1661)
Excluded from local office anyone
Who refused to swear oaths of non-resistance
And allegiance (full marks for persistence),
To take the Anglican sacrament (again)
And to jump through certain other hoops. In vain
Did Charles protest (for I assure you he did).
Officers were forced to declare invalid
The Solemn League and Covenant. That old thing!

It had a distinctly messianic ring,
The whole affair. Then, in 1662,
Came the Act of Uniformity. If you,
Or I, held a position of trust
As a Church minister, or earned a crust
As a schoolteacher, or lectured, perhaps,
At a university, we good chaps –
Dedicated scholars for years and years –
Would all be fired, thrown out on our ears,
Had we not signed up (or so it appears)
To the Anglican Church. Heavens above,
It defies belief. When push came to shove,
A fifth of those folk lost their livelihoods –
No joke: their livings, their lodgings, their goods.

And yet still the Anglicans turned the screw.
The Convention Act (this was quite new)
Forbade all assemblies of five or more
From worshipping (strictly against the law)
Save in accordance with the Prayer Book.
As for the Five Mile Act, go take a look.

The measure was so regressive, so mean,
So stupid – I find it almost obscene.

Charles didn't approve. I'm certain of that.
He made many attempts, off his own bat,
To mitigate the dreadful damage done
By these new laws – rotten, every one.
Sadly, he failed, which only goes to show
That plain good sense had a long way to go.
The King's Declarations of Indulgence,
Bless him, we can conjure in his defence,
But time and again they were thrown out
By the Commons. I've not the slightest doubt
It was fear of Papists (I've said it before)
That inflamed their spirits, and this I deplore.

Money and finance

It should already have become pretty clear
That the King's powers were limited. Oh, dear.
True, he retained the right to dismiss, at will,
The Commons, but he didn't try this until
(Believe it or not) 1679.
They rubbed along most uneasily. Well, fine.
The main problem, however, the bottom line,
The crucial issue that caused greatest grief,
As ever, was finance. It's my firm belief
That no government in British history
Has had enough money. It's no mystery.
Promises, good intentions, aspirations,
Have ever led to turbulent relations –
First between sovereign and Parliament,
Then (come democracy) between government
And the people. Those who make these grand pledges
(After protecting their own privileges)
Find themselves powerless, more often than not,
To deliver. Politicians, a rum lot,
Promise the moon, but it's so much tommyrot.

Rhyming History

"*Plus ça change,*" say the French, "*plus c'est la même chose.*"
If you can't translate, please find someone who knows.

For where money's concerned, men are at their worst.
Charles was delighted (who wouldn't be?), at first,
By an undertaking by Parliament
To make him, effectively, independent
Of their favour, with an income guaranteed
(This was explicit) for life. The sum agreed
Was one million, two hundred thousand pounds –
That's *per annum*, of course. The figure astounds.

However, things were not as they first appeared.
A large share of the King's income disappeared
Once his own expenditure (a huge amount)
Had been factored in. Taking into account
His mistresses (they all needed 'attention'),
His progeny (positively Lawrentian),
His palaces… oh, and I'd better mention
His regal garments (he was King, after all),
His coronation… If Charles were to walk tall,
As the people expected, he had to spend.
Where, his ministers fretted, would it all end?

Nobody vetted the King's expenditure –
At least, not at first. Robes of velvet and fur,
Ermine and silk… His coronation alone
Cost a pretty penny. "Give a dog a bone…"
As the saying goes. Give the people a King,
They want silver, gold, jewels, everything.
Not only did Charles lay out more than he had,
The sums he was promised (this all rather sad)
Altogether failed to materialise.
What Charles, in his wisdom, failed to realise
Was that Parliament was fairly inept
When it came to figures. The King was in debt
Within a year. Outlay exceeded income
By hundreds of thousands of pounds – quite a sum!

One million, two hundred thousand pounds? Well,
He saw eighty *per cent* of that, truth to tell,
And only then if he was lucky. Enough.
Economics? Terminally boring stuff.

Coronation   1661

As intimated, the King's coronation
Was a great event that inspired the nation.

It took place in April, 1661 –
On the 23rd, to be exact. The sun
Shone that day (St. George's Day). The bishops wore
Gold copes. At Westminster Abbey (the west door),
Charles was met by nobility by the score,
The peers in their robes, holding their coronets.
Fine anthems were sung. No one was placing bets

Rhyming History

On the length of his reign. Yet, on this glad day,
Old, unhappy memories were stashed away,
As his Majesty made his way to the throne.

With no Queen, he must have felt rather alone.
Not that he showed it. Charles was in his element.
He heard the Bishop of London ask all present –
 "Lift up your hearts!" he cried – whether they would accept
Charles for their King or no. The tender-hearted wept.
Four times they shouted, "God save King Charles the Second!"
His coronation was generally reckoned
One of the grandest (and most costly) of all time.
I feel privileged to celebrate it in rhyme.

The King was anointed. Well, he had to be –
That was the key point of the ceremony.
His waistcoat was opened "in divers places,"
Evelyn tells us (they loosened the laces,
I imagine). The Bishop "commodiously"
Anointed the palms of his hands, for all to see;
Then his breast; then "twixt the shoulders"; then, finally,
The "crown of his head". You almost feel you were there,
An eye-witness. Then they smoothed down the royal hair
As the Imperial Crown was placed on his head.

The peers of the realm knew their place, it has to be said.
Only now did they don their coronets. A ring
Was slipped, with reverence, on Charles' finger. Singing
Of more anthems followed, music with viols, lutes
And trumpets. The choir, in their best Sunday suits,
Led a rendition of the splendid *Te Deum*.

There were republicans who cursed the tedium
Of this ritual; who hoped for that happy day
When this royalist nonsense would be swept away.
But these disappointed spoilsports, with good reason,
Were given the cold shoulder, well out of season.

Charles the Second and the Restoration

His Majesty received the Holy Sacrament –
Another sore point if you harboured discontent –
Before sailing, by "triumphal barge", to Whitehall,
Where extraordinary feasting crowned it all.

The next day John Evelyn presented the King
With "his panegyric". It does set one thinking:
All that praise; that flattery. A pretty cool head
Had the King. He was a man not easily led,
For he knew his own mind and he died in his bed.

Marriage

The King was badly in need of an heir.
There was consternation, everywhere,
At the conduct of Charles' younger brother,
James, Duke of York. He'd 'met' (under cover)
Old Clarendon's daughter, the lively Anne.

Marriage, however, wasn't the plan.
Anne Hyde was cool, attractive and witty.
James seduced her and she, more's the pity,
Fell pregnant. Clarendon was furious,
Wanted her head chopped off! I'm curious
Why he felt so strongly – perhaps to show,
Though her dad, that he'd not been 'in the know'?
The sad Earl was heavily criticised –
And this he surely must have realised –
For seeking to get closer to the throne
By marrying off Anne (one of his own)
To the arrogant Duke, the first in line.
James, it emerged, had second thoughts, the swine,
And sought to dump the poor lass, now with child.
Charles, to his credit, was mightily riled.
He liked Anne and refused to harry her
(Unlike others). He made James marry her!

Rhyming History

The irony, of course, despite these 'scenes',
Is that Mary and Anne both became Queens –
Anne's two daughters. How wonderful is that?
But if that was the plan, I'll eat my hat.

Despite Anne's later popularity –
The Duchess was a hit at Court, you see –
James' marriage made people suspicious
Of his judgement. Rumours, too (quite vicious),
Were circulating (which proved to be true)
Of his Catholic tendencies. Who knew,
Was the whispered question, what would occur
Should Charles die without issue? They'd prefer
Henry, the third brother, to have been King –
Protestant to his bones. But he, poor thing,
The "sweet" Duke of Gloucester, had lately died –
A sore loss indeed, it can't be denied.
Sturdy and fit, he'd suffered the smallpox,
"In prime of youth". England were on the rocks
Should the King succumb to the same disease,
As well he might. Their sister, if you please,
Mary of Orange, contracted it too
And died. Simply no cure. What could you do?

Distrust of Catholics was nothing new,
But should James succeed... a Catholic *coup*?
This people feared. The solution, in short,
Was to find Charles a Queen! Get her to Court!

The choice fell on Catherine of Braganza,
From Portugal. Something of a bonanza
Was the huge dowry that the *Infanta*
Brought to the table. Charles couldn't have cared less,
Of course, for her wealth – though, I have to confess,
He was reported "very much affected"
When her assets were listed! As expected,
He found the three hundred thousand pounds (in cash)
Not unpalatable. He'd have been most rash,

Charles the Second and the Restoration

Rash indeed, to have turned his back on Bombay
And the port of Tangier (though, I have to say,
The latter caused many a headache). One day,
If I've time, I'll have more to say about that.

The *Infanta* was tiny, like a wee bat,
But not unappealing. She was twenty-three
(On the old side), renowned for her piety
(On the plus side), and, though she had sticky-out teeth
(On the plain side), it was Charles' confirmed belief,
Once he had seen her, that she'd nothing in her face
That "can shock one". In short, she was no disgrace.
In fact, the King thought her eyes were "excellent good".
If anyone would do for a Queen, she would.

Spain was far from pleased, for Portugal, you see,
Was Spain's bitter and long-standing enemy.

Rhyming History

Philip the Fourth complained vociferously,
But Charles remained unmoved. The French, conversely,
Were delighted, as the friendship between Spain
(Their age-old foe) and England began to wane.
King Charles, in fact, had everything to gain,
And little to lose, in mending relations
With his cousin Louis, considerations
Regarding the Dutch uppermost in his mind –
A prime concern. Charles wasn't being unkind
When he described his fair wife as "no beauty".
Catherine did her best to do her duty
And proved (in my view) something of a cutie.

The new Queen

Catherine arrived in May '62.   **1662**
A Catholic consort was nothing new.
Few could remember (curious, but true)
Anyone else but a Catholic Queen.
Anne of Denmark was Protestant – had been,
At least (James the First's long-suffering wife),
Before she converted early in life.
Anne kept her head down. Her daughter-in-law
Was the opposite, though. This I deplore.
Henrietta Maria, Charles' mother,
Was vastly unpopular – oh, brother!

She sought to convert not only her sons –
Charles, James and Henry, all her little ones –
But exerted a malign influence
Over Charles the First, her husband. Good sense
Prevailed with Henry and Charles (the younger),
But with James (call me a rumour monger)
His mother's charisma (witchcraft, some said)
Worked its wicked magic. After she'd fled,
To France, early on in the Civil War,
She ruled the roost. That's what mothers were for,

She crowed. James, poor fool, fell into her trap,
But Charles and Henry (a sensible chap)
Stuck to their Protestant roots, resisted
Their mother's wiles and, though James 'enlisted',
Held aloof from Rome. The old Queen lost face
As the years rolled on. Now a burnt-out case,
Her Catholic character caused no one,
But no one, to fret. Where no one once dared
To cross Henrietta, now no one cared.

Rather a roundabout way to explain
Why poor old England, when faced yet again
With a popish Queen, and foreign to boot,
Simply shrugged her shoulders. Who gave a hoot?
In the case of Catherine, anyway,
Charles won the assurance that, come what may,
She would never attempt to interfere
In affairs of state – nor did she, the dear!

The King and his new bride were 'married' twice:
A Catholic service to break the ice
(To satisfy the Queen), in secrecy,
Private and necessarily low key;
Then a full, Protestant ceremony,
Open and plain for the people to see.

Catherine brought an ample retinue
Of Portuguese servants (well, wouldn't you?):
Ladies-in-waiting (ugly as sin
The lot of them, of ancient origin),
Monks, dressmakers, acrobats, hairdressers,
Cooks, dancing-masters, father-confessors…
For reasons that will later become clear,
This rag-bag of attendants (dear, oh dear)
Didn't last long. But what's important here
Is that the *Infanta* tried, from day one,
To live the English way. Everyone,

Rhyming History

From the start, admired the Portuguese Queen –
Well, not Barbara Palmer, as we've seen,
Nor Andrew Marvell, the poet. I mean,
To call the Queen "a goblin" – how obscene.
I had high admiration for Marvell.
A fallen poet. How tragic. Ah, well…

The Queen arrived at last at Hampton Court
On the 29th of May. Now this ought,
By rights, to have been a merry event.
For Charles paid Catherine the compliment
Of welcoming her 'home' on his birthday,
Co-incident with the very same day,
Two years before, as his Restoration.
Evelyn was there. His fascination
Shines through. He notes the "monstrous fardingals"
Of the "Portuguese ladies" (the Queen's pals) –
All "sufficiently unagreeable"
(The ladies, he means). Unforeseeable,
To Evelyn, was how short a time they'd last!

Portraits suggest that Cath had a slight cast
(Or so it looks to me) in her right eye,
Yet John singles out (and I wonder why –
I have to say, it comes as a surprise)
Her fine "languishing and excellent eyes".
As for her hair, she wore "her foretop long" –
The Portuguese way, though I could be wrong –
"And turned aside very strangely". She changed,
However, within weeks. Her hair's arranged,
In all her pictures, in the English style.
She quickly proved herself an Anglophile.

A nasty shock lay in store, however,
For the Queen. Charles had been less than clever
In installing his favourite mistress,
'You-Know-Who' (husbands have been hanged for less),

Charles the Second and the Restoration

In her very own private apartment
At Hampton Court. It's not my department –
I'm a humble poet, not a critic –
But in my judgement: less than terrific!
Clumsy, callous, unthinking, unfeeling,
The whole affair left Catherine reeling.
Oh, and one thing I forgot to tell you:
The Lady Castlemaine was pregnant, too,
With her second child (both the King's, of course).

Catherine's first reaction was storm force,
Particularly when Charles sought (the cheek)
To foist his mistress on the Queen (so weak)
As a lady-in-waiting. She refused,
To her credit. She felt roundly abused.
But when she got tricked into meeting Babs
(The Queen was new; she could hardly keep tabs
On everyone), Catherine passed out.
Castlemaine, it seemed, had won the first bout.

Yet the ex-*Infanta* was no weakling.
For better or worse the wife of the King,
She settled on a strategy. Her train
Was dismissed, causing misery and strain
To the lonely Queen. She made up her mind.
Her husband was hers. He might be unkind,
Unfaithful and selfish and unrefined,
But that was Charles. She'd better believe it.
She'd only one choice: take it or leave it.

She gathered her wits. She changed in a trice.
She swallowed her pride, was even quite nice
(When the need arose) to Barbara P.
She judged Charles' character down to a T.
It wasn't a choice between 'her' and 'me' –
Both he'd enjoy. So she dressed sexily,
Raised the hems of her skirts for Charles to see,

And was even known, occasionally,
To flash him a bit (just a hint) of knee.

I'm egging the oyster, evidently,
But you get the gist. Between you and me,
I admire the Queen. She could have been sad –
And she must, at times, have been far from glad –
Yet she made the most of her life. Not bad.

So then, though far from satisfactory
(A tainted sort of domesticity),
Let's leave the Queen, still in the royal bed
(Just), and turn to foreign affairs instead.

The Dutch and the French   1664

There was pressure on the King from all quarters
To declare war on the Dutch – choppy waters,

Charles the Second and the Restoration

Believe you me. Commercial rivalry
Was at its height. Our trading supremacy
Was at stake. The conflict, in reality,
Was well under way, for there wasn't that much
To prevent us taking a pot at the Dutch.
On the eastern coast of North America,
And all down the western side of Africa,
There were bloody sea battles, fought to the death.
The Dutch were fighting to their very last breath
When New Amsterdam fell (rechristened New York).

There were those who dismissed the Dutch as all talk –
A serious error. A great victory
In the West African country of Guinea,
And other lesser 'triumphs' (though who are we
To gloat, given that Guinea, undoubtedly,
Was mixed up in the foul trade of slavery?),
Gave rise to an overweening certainty
That the English were invincible. Not all,
To be sure, were completely comfortable
With the prospect of open conflict. The squall
Could fast become a tempest, the price too dear.

Pepys dreaded it, as his *Diary* makes clear,
But when war was declared, a rousing "Hear, hear!"
Was the dominant voice. The King had delayed
As long as he could. He'd been faintly dismayed
(Disappointed, too) by a Franco-Dutch pact
To isolate Spain. This discomforting fact
Was a fly in the ointment (I'd best explain)
In Charles' own plan to favour France over Spain.
It's all rather complex. He'd have much preferred
An alliance with France, but that, in a word,
Had been scuppered by Louis. Charles, at a glance,
Should have seen it in capitals: NEVER TRUST FRANCE!

Be that as it may, the momentum was such
That the King, at last, declared war on the Dutch.

Rhyming History

Was the cheering too loud? I'd say, just a touch.
The English rejoiced, but a little too much.

Where the funds were expected to come from exactly,
The Commons, as ever, were frustratingly vague. He,
Charles, put his trust in Parliament to support him,
Overlooking for now the trouble they'd brought him.

The King took a personal interest
In the war. Charles was at his very best
In matters nautical. He expected
The highest of standards and inspected,
In person, his fleet, warships and their crews,
Over a hundred in number – great news.
20,000 men (whatever your views)
Are quite a Navy; and 4,000 guns
Was certain to give those Dutchmen the runs.

Sam Pepys knew better. As Clerk of the Acts
(A naval appointment) he had the facts.
A large number of the sailors, alas,
Had been press-ganged. It was verging on crass
To boast of a crack, well-disciplined force.
There was then the issue of cash, of course.
The sailors were not so much underpaid
As unpaid. While grandiose plans were laid
To punish the Dutch, the men, it appears,
Were focused on other concerns – arrears!

Pepys had first-hand knowledge too (through his job)
Of profiteering. If it cost a bob,
He'd be billed for a crown – the King, that is.
Charles footed the bill. Pepys could (in a tizz)
Himself cook the books, exaggerating –
Though he'd surely call it 'overstating' –
Specific sums laid out on equipment,
To goad a tight-fisted Parliament

Charles the Second and the Restoration

Into voting the funds. Close as they were,
The Commons coughed up with little demur.
Corruption? Certainly not in Pepys' case.
'Leverage', I'd call it. That's no disgrace.
The Commons needed a kick up the arse –
They promised the moon, but gave nothing. A farce.

James, Duke of York, was Commander of the Fleet,
Lord High Admiral. The Duke had found his feet,
Aboard ship, as a boy. He adored the sea.
It was his element and, it seems to me
(Though no royalist myself), his appointment
Was inspired and caused little disappointment.

An engagement off Lowestoft, in mid-June,
Gave good cause for the cynics to change their tune.

Rhyming History

Pepys records the battle in graphic detail,
Although absent himself. Nobody could fail
To be impressed: a glorious victory –
One of our country's most decisive at sea.
Twenty-four of the finest ships of the Dutch
Were taken or sunk. Casualties were such
That the numbers (vast) could scarce be recorded –
Between eight and ten thousand. This afforded
Great rejoicing, given that the English dead
Numbered a mere two hundred. Richard Doyle's head
(Now here's a striking detail) flew through the air
And landed on James (the Duke, yes, the King's heir),
Felling him to the deck. Doyle was one of three,
Struck by a single shot and killed instantly.

Their "blood and brains," Pepys informs us with relish,
Flew in James' face. We know warfare is hellish,
But it serves us well, just occasionally,
To be shown how bad. It reminds us, you see,
And wrestles us out of our complacency.
No foreign reporters then, no BBC –
Just Pepys, bless him. Evelyn lends a nice touch:
The Duke of York's dog (I treasure this so much)
Sought out on board "the very securest place…
"When they were in fight". Fine, but what a disgrace
To take your dog to war. Think of the terror!
The gunfire! The din! A terrible error.

Death enjoyed a field day at Lowestoft,
Yet with tears in my eyes (I'm growing soft)
I conjure now a greater tragedy.
It's not enough simply to be sad, you see,
For now we must weep, and weep copiously.

The Great Plague   1665

Plague had ever lurked in London's crowded streets,
Its narrow lanes and byways, its dark retreats,

Charles the Second and the Restoration

Its busy passages, its wide, stinking drains
And open sewers. From what one ascertains,
There was no connection drawn (bizarre, but true)
Between hygiene and disease. Let me tell you,
I'm glad to be living in a later age.
The Plague, just imagine… Read on, down the page…

Pepys again is our day-to-day eye-witness:
Seven months of danger, terror and distress.

June the 7th Pepys jotted in his *Diary*:
"The hottest day that ever I felt." Fiery,
Blistering, it was London's dire misfortune
That the summer was such a scorcher. 'Flaming' June

Rhyming History

Gave way to record temperatures in July,
And then through August into September. That's why,
Alas, the awful Plague was able to take hold,
The worst instance of the pestilence, so we're told,
In London's history. Pepys, on this fateful day,
Was strolling, no care in the world (as was his way),
Down Drury Lane, when he spotted (alackaday)
"Two or three houses marked with a red cross", the first
"To my remembrance". Samuel feared the worst.
Red crosses on the doors! The capital was cursed!

June the 10th Pepys reports (more's the pity)
"That the Plague is come into the City".
Worse still, it had fetched up in Fenchurch Street,
In the house (Pepys' heart must have missed a beat)
Of Dr. Burnett, his neighbour and friend.
The good Doctor contemplated his end,
Alone. According to his chum's record,
He shut himself up "of his own accord".
One hopes that virtue reaped its just reward:
Most generous to his neighbours, and some!
As Pepys comments aptly, "very handsome".

By immuring himself, the Doctor, no doubt,
Was hoping the pestilence wouldn't get out.
The authorities later enforced a law
That infected families (mainly the poor,
Inevitably) should be made to remain
Boarded up in their houses. Picture the strain,
The stress, the despair, as they waited for Death,
Clawing at the walls till their very last breath.
The rich and the powerful (this I deplore)
Evaded this cruel (though practical) law,
By fleeing to the country. Need I say more?
What else, they would argue, was affluence for?

Pepys, like Evelyn, his fellow diarist,
Stayed in the City, a point that's often missed.

Charles the Second and the Restoration

No, to be fair, towards the end of the year
Pepys decamped out of London. But with the fear,
The uncertainty, and the ever present
Dread of infection, who are we to resent
His decision? What people did find galling
Was the conduct of the Court: quite appalling!
The Queen 'emigrated' to Salisbury,
And when one of her grooms' wives (poor woman, she)
Succumbed to the disease, they set off again,
For Milton – Queen, Court and her entire train.
Charles, fair to say, remained in London longer,
Together with James, both fitter and stronger.
I do have to say, this was reckless and rash.
He was King, after all, and didn't lack cash.
Cowardice in the mighty is never nice,
But for Charles to die? A senseless sacrifice.

June the 14th One hundred and twelve died
"This last week". The figure, a rising tide,
Compared with forty-three the week before.
For forty-six long weeks Pepys kept a score,
The increase in numbers terrifying.
Yet he moved in the midst, death defying!

June the 17th Pepys was in a coach –
His bravery is far beyond reproach,
Given the patent risk of infection –
Driving in an easterly direction,
Down Holborn, when the coachman suddenly
Was "struck very sick" so "he could not see".
Pepys switched coaches (quite understandably),
Dreading the Plague. This was how it began,
With a sneeze and falling sickness. The man,
Pepys feared (a witness to his sudden fit),
Was "struck with the Plague". Would he now catch it?

A mass exodus from London began,
By coach, by wagon, by barge. Some just ran!

Rhyming History

John Evelyn stayed for the duration.
A hero, he never left his station
As Charles' commissioner for the care
Of sick and wounded prisoners. Despair,
Panic and cowardice were not for John.
As the Plague raged about him, he pressed on,
Loyal, determined, with a job to do
In the King's service. He trusted (would you?)
"In the prudence and the goodness of God".

A dangerous path John Evelyn trod.
He reports that he passed "coffins exposed
"In the streets". It can only be supposed
That he was fearless. Upright and devout,
He walked untouched, all too aware, no doubt,
Of his mortality, yet well prepared
To meet his Maker. While others despaired,
He wrote (with an eerie objectivity)
Of the "mournful silence" and, ominously,
"As not knowing whose turn might be next" – and this
At the height of the pestilence; hit or miss
Whether a man lived or died; two thousand dead
In a week. Where most folk of quality fled –
Even Pepys, at the Plague's worst, as we've noted –
Evelyn, bless him, stuck it out, devoted
To the King's cause. I'm pleased (and relieved) to say
That once the threat abated (oh, happy day!)
Our hero was introduced to the King.

Charles ran to greet him (highly gratifying),
Offered his royal hand to kiss and, with grace,
Thanked his good servant for his care in the face
Of such manifest peril. So, no disgrace!

July was also unbearably hot.
The sweltering heat wave, like it or not,

Charles the Second and the Restoration

Fed the infection. Seven hundred died
In the week of the 13th. Suicide
It was to venture abroad. The Plague spread
From parish to parish – one thousand dead
The following week; by the 31st
Near twice that number; still not at its worst.

July the 26th Pepys was afraid.
He aired his concerns. What plans could be made
To put his affairs (both body and soul)
In some sort of order? Upon the whole,
Who can blame the poor wretch? For sure, not I.
He certainly thought he was like to die.

July the 30th This is depressing.
"It was a sad noise to hear our bell to ring
"And toll so often today." Pepys counted five –
No, six times. Would no one be left alive?

August the 8th Here a personal touch:
"Poor Will" (whom, it seems, Pepys liked very much)
"Who used to sell us ale at the hall door" –
Dead, along with his family of four
(Wife and three children) in a single day.
The news strengthened Pepys' resolve, anyway,
Not to venture through the City again.

August the 10th Dread figures. It was plain
The pestilence had still not reached its peak:
Three thousand victims in a single week.
These were too many to be buried at night.
The dead had now to be taken by daylight,
Corpses on carts in the streets a common sight.
On the 15th Pepys met one in an alley,
Being borne down some short steps. Did he dally?
No, sir! Yet he was "not much disturbed at it"
Or, if he was, he wrote not a word of it.

Rhyming History

Rumours abounded how to fight the pestilence.
Chewing tobacco was one way (complete nonsense).
Another, more desperate measure (now, mark this)
Was, however far-fetched, to contract syphilis!

The brothels were full to overflowing. Be sure,
This so-called cure was championed by the 'impure'.
Others reckoned that the Plague travelled 'on the air',
So that bonfires came to be lit everywhere,
On the hottest of days even, outside those doors
Daubed with red crosses. This helped the inmates indoors
Not a jot. The very last thing they now needed
Was heat, the poor beggars. Their cries went unheeded.

Charles the Second and the Restoration

Quite sensibly, a curfew was set in place
By the Lord Mayor: no man to show his face
Outside his house after nine o'clock at night.
This gave the sick the freedom, before first light,
"To go abroad for air" – a humane measure
In those terrible times, and one to treasure.

August the 25th Dr. Burnett,
Pepys' respected chum, had been firmly set,
As we've seen, on protecting his good friends
And neighbours (I hope God pays dividends)
By shutting up his house. His man had died
Weeks before, yet the Doctor had defied
Death (for sure, from the start, his master plan):
"Now himself dead. Poor, unfortunate man!"

August the 31st Two thousand dead.
That, at least, is what Samuel Pepys said.

On the same day (I must say, I'm amazed)
"Our fleet gone out" (evidently unfazed
By events in London) "to find the Dutch".
The war was still going strong and, as such,
Was the usual drain on resources.
I know it's one of my hobbyhorses,
But at a time like this… Beyond belief!
The King, if not careful, would come to grief.
The money, to be blunt, just wasn't there –
England "not in a condition to spare"
(Pepys' phrase), and contagion everywhere.
A recipe, surely, for disaster –
And the death count rising ever faster.

September the 3rd Pepys had a passion,
It seems, for clothes, a figure of fashion.
On this day (Lord's day) he put on his suit,
"Coloured silk… very fine", a wig to boot:

Rhyming History

"My new periwig". Now, Pepys hadn't dared
To don this before. He'd been frankly scared,
For "the Plague had been in Westminster" then –
That is, when he bought it. Ten out of ten
For caution! By September, it appears,
His vanity had overcome his fears.
Be that as it may. Dread of infection,
However, led him to this reflection.
Once the Plague was done, "nobody will dare"
(So he imagines) "to buy any hair…
"For fear that it had been cut off the heads
"Of people dead of the Plague". Disease spreads,
Marked Pepys, *via* men's periwigs. The trend
For wigs would falter. And where would that end?

In the midst of death Pepys could speculate,
Fearlessly, on fashion. At any rate,
He kept his pecker up. People had to.
A bit like the Blitz. What else could they do?

Crowds would come to gawp (edifying, eh?)
At the burials. It grieves me to say,
But mass graves became the order of the day
(Sheer numbers, alas) in unconsecrated ground,
With plunder aplenty for the poor, I'll be bound.
Body-stripping increased the rate of infection –
Rich pickings indeed, with no risk of detection.

September the 14th The first good news.
Five hundred fewer deaths. Who could refuse
To celebrate? Well, Samuel for one.
For within the City, all said and done,
The figures increased, alarmingly near
To Pepys' own home. Little wonder his fear
Went unchecked. He met "dead corpses" close by,
Borne through Fenchurch Street. No need to ask why
He lived in dread of contagion. What's more,
On that same day, with his own eyes, he saw

Charles the Second and the Restoration

"A person sick of the sores", carried close
In a coach, with purulent ulcers. Gross!

September the 20th A cold spell,
Which optimists had hoped would augur well,
Proved a sad and cruel disappointment.
An increase of six hundred cases meant
Over seven thousand deaths in one week,
The highest number ever (by a squeak).
"Nobody but poor wretches in the streets,"
Writes Pepys. At every corner he meets,
To his horror, "corpses of the Plague"; dead
Taken for burial; beggars ill fed
And "sick of the sores"; up and down Whitehall,
Grass growing; on the Thames, no boats at all.

October witnessed deaths in steep decline.
Some weeks marked sudden increases. Well, fine,
But the trend was surely and sharply down.
In one entry, "at our end of the town"
Pepys notes a small but significant rise,
But an overall fall (quite a surprise)
Of seven hundred and forty. He tries
(Who wouldn't?) to keep upbeat and cheerful,
But the facts speak for themselves. It's fearful,
But the folk of Westminster were bereft:
No joke, just one apothecary left
And "never a physician" – all dead,
Apart from some senior figures, who fled.

During November numbers ebbed and flowed,
But London's most pestilent episode
Was drawing to a close. Thanks be to God,
But a mere three hundred and thirty-odd
Perished in the month's dying days. Relief
Was palpable. But Death, that fickle thief,
Robbed Pepys, alas, of his Aunt Bell. Oh, boy –
This news on the day that he wrote, with joy,

Rhyming History

Of the drop in fatalities. The talk
(Huge excitement) of the "wagon" from York
(Hurrah!) "full of passengers" served to show
That London, at last, was back on the go.

At the year's end Samuel Pepys takes stock.
On the stroke of midnight, at twelve o'clock,
He records (here I don't exaggerate),
"To my great joy", a rise in his estate
From thirteen hundred pounds, over the year,
To four thousand, four hundred. Any fear
Of the Plague (still active) takes second place
To his economic concerns. No trace
Of languor or self-pity do we find,
No anger at Fate's *diktat*. He was kind
To his family, incurring great expense
In lodging them at Woolwich, perfect good sense.

Pepys himself took up residence in Greenwich,
Leaving one maid in London. He became rich,
Meanwhile, through the course of this terrible year,
Not only as Treasurer for Tangier
(A new post), but also (whatever this is)
As 'Surveyor of the Victuals'! Gee whizz,
He's a cool customer. His whole family
"Hath been kept well all this while". Easy to see
How Pepys managed to survive this living hell:
Sang froid, pure and simple. "Saving my Aunt Bell,
"Who is dead", his nearest and dearest did well
(With the most sorry exception, sad to tell,
Of his cousin Sarah's children). Many were dead,
"Such as I know very well". How Pepys' heart bled.

The Great Plague was God's punishment for sin,
So thought our honest friend, John Evelyn.
On August the 2nd a solemn fast
Was observed through England. From first to last,

John believed that it was God's displeasure
That carried the Plague and, for good measure,
His disaffection at the current war
Against the dreadful Dutch. What was God for,
If not to visit on us lesser men
A vile contagion every now and then?

Not surprisingly, the pestilence spread
To other towns and cities. York, it's said,
Suffered most grievously and Cambridge too.
Compared to London, the victims were few –
Though outside the walls of York you can see,
Today, the sites of Plague pits. Patently,
York was a serious casualty.

Eyam in Derbyshire earned lasting fame –
A little village, it still made its name –
By willingly (nay, voluntarily)
Shutting its gates and doors, amazingly,
Against the world outside. Eyam, you see,

Rhyming History

Was visited by Plague. The only way
To save its neighbours (it's hard to convey,
In words, the sacrifice) was to hold fast,
United, and see how long it could last.
The brave souls of Eyam should be deified.
Some eighty *per cent* of the villagers died.
The rest of Derbyshire escaped scot free,
A better example, it seems to me,
Of our ancestors' deep humanity
Than the awful instance quoted by Pepys.
This is an outrage and gives me the creeps.
He was witness to "ill people… in spite"
Breathing on the faces (in broad daylight),
"Out of the windows", of the healthy folk
As they passed in the street. No word of a joke.

How many perished in total? Who knows?
Fewer in number than you might suppose,
Given the devastating virulence
Of the infection. I've tried to make sense
Of the statistics. Estimates are rough.
Historians are guessing (fair enough),
But I've read (and this seems far from absurd)
That of all Londoners up to one third
Succumbed. That represents, sorry to tell,
Some hundred thousand hapless victims. Well,
These are figures on which it's painful to dwell.

The Dutch war

The King returned in 1666,   **1666**
The beginning of Feb. In a rare fix,
For the first time in his colourful reign,
He was sorely in need of help. The strain
Of the Dutch war was telling. The struggle
Limped along, a catalogue of muddle,
Lack of cash, the odd win here, defeat there.
A long-drawn-out war, the King was aware,

Charles the Second and the Restoration

Was not what he wanted. Should France declare
On the side of the Dutch – prospect: despair!
Well, she did. And England won no support
From a whole range of quarters. Charles paid court
To Spain, Portugal – trawling for allies
Through all Europe. He failed. What a surprise!
Why should other countries risk life and limb
To tangle with France for the likes of him?

When the French did declare hostilities –
A move which frankly gave him the willies –
The King was obliged (what choice had he got?)
To divide his Navy. Like it or not,
Fear of invasion from France (a long shot,
But far from impossible) forced his hand
And weakened him further, you understand.

One part split off to patrol the French coast,
Under Prince Rupert; the rest, the foremost,
Under our old friend George Monck (back at sea,
As Duke of Albemarle), valiantly
Squared up to the Dutch, the old enemy.

Pepys was pessimistic. He could have cried.
His common sense (he was amply supplied)
Served him well. He didn't like it one bit.
"God knows how little we are fit for it,"
He wrote, when France declared. From where I sit,
He was right. Though the Swedes joined on our side
(In April), the war looked like suicide.

The King quickly had to swallow his pride.
The Dutch gave our lads a pretty rough ride.
On June the 1st the Four Days' Battle, so-called,
Commenced and was fought to the death. I'm appalled,
I confess, at the reports. For what mattered
Were the losses – our fleet "miserably shattered,"

Rhyming History

Wrote Evelyn, "hardly a vessel entire".
One can only surmise that John (a live wire)
Was depressed; some ten or eleven ships lost,
"And near 600 men slain", a massive cost.
It seems, indeed, that he was conservative
In his estimates. The numbers, as I live,
Grossly exceeded his tally. This I've read:
Upward of 5,000 English sailors dead;
Many others hideously maimed or burnt.
Some 2,000 Dutch perished. Were lessons learnt?
Were morals drawn? Warnings heeded? Were they heck!
The English fleet, a smouldering, mangled wreck,
Was back in action as early as July.
It beggars belief. One can only ask, why?
"Revenge on the Hollanders!" A rousing cry,
That hoary old standby: "To do, or die!"

Truth to tell, the war was fast reaching stalemate.
Yet peace talks, I'm sad to say, would have to wait.
King Charles was now poised for his third brush with Fate!

The Great Fire

According to our good friend, John Evelyn,
The Great Fire of London's site of origin
Was "near Fish Street". Some say this was Pudding Lane,
A neighbouring byway. There's little to gain,
Perhaps, by indulging in speculation,
But all are agreed that the conflagration
Began on Sunday, September the 2nd,
In a bake house (it's generally reckoned)
On the edge of the City, just to the east
Of London Bridge. Nobody (at first, at least)
Seemed unduly alarmed. Fire was commonplace.
At 3 a.m. one of Pepys' maids (just in case)
Woke up her master and bade him take a look.
He was too unconcerned by far, in my book.

Charles the Second and the Restoration

Seething Lane was just a quarter-mile or so
From the seat of the fire – a mere stone's throw.
That was enough (or rather it should have been)
To warn him. But this wasn't the worst he'd seen,
So he went back to bed to finish his kip.

Yet the flames soon had the City in their grip.
Already, by daylight, the whole of Fish Street
Was ablaze and around London Bridge the heat
Was intense, with (according to Jane, the maid)
Three hundred houses lost. Pepys was now dismayed.
He secured a vantage point on the Tower,
Whence he saw the force of the fire grow, hour
By hour, minute by… nay, by the second.
Action was needed! Calamity beckoned!

Rhyming History

Evelyn witnessed it from the south bank
And, as usual, we have him to thank
For his telling description. The wind fanned
The flames. Londoners, it seemed, were unmanned
By the "fierce eastern wind". Quite out of hand,
The fire raged on. A "very dry season"
Was also, for sure, part of the reason.
The fact of the easterly wind explains
Why Pepys' house escaped. For all of his pains,
His place would have been consumed in the face
Of a wind from the west. Yet now, apace,
He resolved to act. The King must be told.

Like an old-fashioned knight, fearless and bold,
Pepys wended his way to the waterside –
His calm in a crisis can't be denied –
Took a boat, and was rowed up to Whitehall.

En route what he saw brought no comfort at all,
Nobody making the slightest endeavour
To quench the flames and (this far from clever)
The poor folk remaining in their houses
Till the heat drove them out. This arouses
Pity and horror in equal measure.
One detail from Pepys (and one to treasure,
If cruel) were the wee pigeons. They, too,
Were "loth to leave their houses". Sad, but true,
They fluttered close to the flames, if you please,
Hovering round windows and balconies
"Till they burned their wings and fell down". The King,
Fearful and concerned, ordered anything
That needed doing to be done. Like what,
You may ask? Charles dithered. A foul French plot?
A Dutch conspiracy? Only a clot
Would ignore the odds and, like it or not,
England was at war. So, to stop the rot,
What did the King propose? Diddly-squat!

Charles the Second and the Restoration

Pepys, then, suggested (according to him)
That Charles should order (sorry to be dim,
But obvious or what?), as fire breaks,
Houses to be pulled down, for all their sakes.

The King agreed, commanding Samuel
To order the Mayor (yes, you can tell
How little Charles did himself at this stage)
To spare no dwellings. The fire's horrid rage
Confounded the sad and pitiful Mayor.
The poor chap was but a bit-part player
In the drama. Wet with perspiration,
Meeting Pepys, he vented his frustration:
Few men would obey him, and those who did
Were overtaken by the flames. Well rid
He was of the whole wretched business!
Patently in a state of some distress,
He excused himself. He'd been up all night.
Let somebody else, he said, put it right.
Some Mayor! Woefully lacking in fight.

In desperation, men removed their goods
From their burning homes. Yet out of the woods,
Sad to say, they were not. Let them run fast,
The fire raged faster. An idle task.
They'd move to a safer habitation,
Only to find that the conflagration
Consumed that too, and within the hour.
Citizens struggled with all their power
To save their treasures and best possessions.

Cries of woe, disconsolate expressions
Of grief rent the acrid, smoke-ridden air;
Wagons and carts (gridlock everywhere),
Groaning with goods. Housewives, grim with despair,
Piled their prized belongings into lighters
(River craft). These Londoners were fighters,
But many (the poor, deluded blighters)

Rhyming History

Saw their furniture sink or run aground.
As many as one boat in three, Pepys found –
For he was witness to the sorry sight –
Contained "a pair of virginals". That night,
From Bankside, he beheld the City burn.

Flames licked the houses at every turn.
He observed the fire grow "more and more"
As darkness took hold: churches by the score,
Their steeples ablaze; the tongues of fire
Torching the buildings, higher and higher.

"One entire arch of fire" Pepys now saw,
"Of above a mile long". He watched in awe –
Nay, horror: "It made me weep to see it."
The only recourse was flight. So be it.

Yet Pepys hurried back to his own abode,
The fire by now not far from his road.
He bore some of his best goods "by moonshine"
Into his garden. These would include wine,
I'd hazard (even periwigs?). Well, fine,
Why not? His money and his "iron chests" –
Officials in those days feathered their nests –
He moved to the cellar, the safest place
Should his house be destroyed; and, just in case,
He gathered together his bags of gold –
To take to his office (or so we're told).

The following morning, at four o'clock,
He sent for a cart to remove his 'stock' –
His plate, all his money and his "best things" –
To Bethnal Green. The comings and goings
Were a sight to behold, with all the town
On the move – and Pepys still in his nightgown,
In that cart! The mind boggles. Proud? Not he,
So long as his goods were stashed securely.

Charles the Second and the Restoration

Evelyn again: September the 3rd.
His report that day is to be preferred
To Pepys'. The latter is pre-occupied
(Who can blame him? I'd have been petrified)
With his own safety. Again from Bankside,
John saw "the whole south part of the City",
All of London, ablaze (oh, the pity)
From Cheapside to the Thames, along Cornhill
And, "kindled back" by the south-east wind still,
Now consuming Tower Street, Fenchurch Street
And Gracious Street. This was a mere heartbeat,
Scarily, from Pepys down in Seething Lane –
A fact that goes a long way to explain
His personal forebodings on that day.
I'd have shared his terror, I have to say.

The heat seemed somehow to "ignite the air",
Contriving (quite creepy this), to prepare
The materials to "conceive the fire".
The fierce wind, as we've seen, sought to conspire
With the arid season. The conflagration
Brought upon people a "strange consternation";
There was "crying out and lamentation";
And, according to John's computation,
The "clouds… of smoke" reached "fifty miles in length".
Our own best eye-witness (his greatest strength),
Evelyn notices that "all the sky
"Were of a fiery aspect" (oh, my…)
"Like the top of a burning oven". Night –
"If I may call that night" – became daylight,
Can you believe, "for ten miles round about".

It surely wasn't only the devout
Who feared the wrath of God. John had no doubt.
"A resemblance of Sodom" so it was,
"Or the last day" – and this surely because
No other image sufficed. "London was"

Rhyming History

(Mark Evelyn's sombre words) "but is no more."
Two square miles the fire consumed. Oh, lor!
And still that's only on the second day.
On September the 4th, sorry to say,
The news was no better. Oh, by the way,
I missed from my account of yesterday
The loss of St. Paul's. The fire took hold
As the flames were fanned westward. The "scaffolds,"
John wrote, "contributed exceedingly"
As fire consumed the Church, greedily.

On the morning of September the 4th –
As swarms of refugees were fleeing north –
The King of England finally set forth,
On horseback, his brother James at his side,
To inspect the damage. You can decide
For yourselves the scale of their amazement:
"The lead melting down the streets", the pavement

Charles the Second and the Restoration

"Glowing with fiery redness", the roof
Of St. Paul's a burning, liquid mass – proof
(Were proof required) of God's wrath. For the stones
"Of Pauls flew like grenados" and the bones
Of newly buried bodies crackled and snapped
In their blistering coffins, as Satan clapped,
Crying "*Encore*!" to Death: "Let them suffer again",
The hideous victims of Plague. "More pain! More pain!"

The blaze now spread west as far as St. Bride's –
Fleet Street, Old Bailey, Ludgate Hill besides:
All to ashes. The King rode to and fro,
Distributing silver. Those in the know
Were now of a mind to a policy
Of blowing up properties, which, to me
(As it did to Evelyn), seemed to be
The best and most sensible strategy.
Bring on the gunpowder! Thus, gradually,
The great inferno, through men's industry,
And by God's good grace, lessened its dread fury.

The heat was still intense. A "furlong's space"
Was the distance to save a burning face.
Avoid standing by a "glowing ruin,"
Warned ever sensible John Evelyn.
As he left "this smoking and sultry heap"
With a sad heart (you are welcome to weep),
The "poor inhabitants" of the City
Evelyn saw dispersed (here's a pity)
"All about Moorfields, as far as Highgate" –
Many of them in a pitiful state,
Some in tents, others in hovels and huts,
"Without a rag". This was (no ifs, no buts),
By any standards, a calamity.
An Act of God. A great catastrophe.

The King gained some rare personal credit,
Along with his brother (there, I've said it),

Rhyming History

By rolling up his sleeves, getting stuck in
And doing his bit. As clean as a pin,
He ended up blackened (don't call it spin),
Covered in charcoal and with blistered feet.
His shoes were all burnt, so great was the heat:
A most singular hero, the perspiration
Dripping off his honest brow! An inspiration!

A disaster for the English nation?
Not so, in the end. An explanation
Will follow. For now, the situation
Was bleak. The homelessness, the misery…
But one quite wondrous fact, it seems to me,
Shines through. Barely any citizens died –
A handful. The rest, though, were terrified.
Their courage never ceases to amaze,
And as for counselling… not in those days.

Charles the Second and the Restoration

Pepys tells the story of one little cat,
Rescued from a chimney (how about that?),
His fur burnt off his body… "yet alive".
A marvel how these animals survive.
I dare say Puss was pretty traumatised,
But glad to live or I'd be much surprised.
A happy result, though terribly sad:
Nine lives, and just as well. That's one he'd had!

On Wednesday the 5th (day four, that is)
The raging conflagration lost its fizz.
The blowing up of buildings did the trick.
Once Charles had got the message, he'd been quick
To implement the policy. Too late,
Alas, for some, who'd far too long to wait
And lost their livelihoods, a sorry fate.
"Tenacious and avaricious men,"
Wrote Evelyn in scorn, "like aldermen",
Self-centred and obtuse, were not amused
When such measures were mooted. They refused
To yield. Their houses would have been the first,
So they did "not permit" it. They were cursed,
Roundly cursed. They might well have saved London.
They blew it, and fearful damage was done.

The flames were halted at "Temple westward"
And, to the north (we have Evelyn's word),
At Smithfield. In John's unshakeable view,
The Hospital of St. Bartholomew,
Located close by, was spared by God's grace.
Why He allowed the storm in the first place,
I shall leave you to ponder. However,
The combination of man's endeavour
(Blowing up houses) and better weather
(Abating of the wind) stopped the progress
Of the mighty fire. I should confess,
Were I asked, that God played no part in it.
Tell that to Evelyn and he'd have a fit.

Rhyming History

So the great conflagration, bit by bit,
Burnt itself out. On the 7th (Friday)
Evelyn rose early and made his way
Through the ruins of the once great City.
His description is graphic and gritty.
With "extraordinary difficulty"
He clambered over mountains of debris,
Still smoking as far as the eye could see.

Passing through "the late Fleet Street, Ludgate Hill,
"By St. Paul's, Cheapside" and thence to Cornhill,
He found himself "mistaking where I was" –
Bishopsgate? Aldersgate? – and this because
The landscape was all "smoking rubbish". Yet,
Amazed, John stumbled on, "over in sweat",
His feet so hot, from the soles of his shoes
Burning from the heat of the ground. Grim news:

"A sheet of lead… six acres by measure",
The roof of St. Paul's, the City's treasure,
All melted; its "beautiful portico"
Now rent in pieces; and (there's more to go)
"Near one hundred" churches destroyed beside.
The pity of it cannot be denied.

Rumours abounded of conspiracy.
The Dutch (or the French) had torched the City.
With both "we were now in hostility" –
Evelyn again. So, why ever not?
Catholics, of course, were in on the plot.
His Majesty stepped in to stop the rot.
The reports were false. The gossips were wrong.
He denied them all. Yet the scent was strong!
Years, years later, James, Duke of York (no less),
One of the bravest, I have to confess,
In facing up to the great inferno,
Was charged with starting it! I'm pleased to say, though,
That James, Duke of Monmouth (the young so-and-so),
Was laughed out of court, the lowest of the low.

Evelyn believed that the conflagration
Was God's judgement upon a corrupt nation.
On October the 10th a general fast
Was "indicted", which was witness (at long last)
To how men were humbled by plague and war
(As well as fire). Evelyn knew the score.
These "most dismal judgments" were the consequence
Of the "dissolute Court" (what utter nonsense),
"Burning lusts… prodigious ingratitude…
"Profane and abominable lives". How rude!
To attack the King thus! I'm quite surprised.
John was more straitlaced than I realised.

Six days before the Great Fire took hold,
A select group of worthies (so we're told)

Rhyming History

Met at St. Paul's to inspect the steeple.
That Evelyn himself, of all people,
Should have been of their number intrigues me,
Given the account in his *Diary*
Of its destruction just a week later,
And he a witness and key spectator.
The party included one Dr. Wren,
Along with "several expert workmen",
Clergy from St. Paul's (including the Dean),
And the Bishop of London. Wren was keen,
With Evelyn, to tear the steeple down
(Unstable) and to build a sort of 'crown',
Described as a "Cupola", in its place –
A structure of strange and "wonderful grace",
Unknown in England. All were agreed,
After heated debate, Wren should proceed
With designs for his magnificent Dome.
After drinks with the Bish they trooped off home.

Christopher Wren

Who'd have thought it? In a matter of days
Steeple, and all, were consumed in the blaze.
Christopher Wren was ahead of the game.
The 'man of the moment', he made his name.
It wasn't a case of overnight fame.
Wren was the ripe old age of thirty-four
By the time of the Fire. Civil War
Disrupted his early education.
His family were of the King's 'station',
Taking refuge in rural Oxfordshire.
Chris, as a boy, was quick to aspire
To books and learning. His heart's desire
Was science: arithmetic, geometry
And later, at Oxford, astronomy.
A Fellow of All Souls at twenty-one,
He was quick to earn his place in the sun.

Evelyn met him at dinner one night,
At Wadham, and calls him not only bright,
But "prodigious". That's no flattery.
Wren was Professor of Anatomy,
Just five years later, at Gresham College,
Suggesting a range and depth of knowledge
Extraordinary in one so young.

Yet he occupied still a lowly rung
On the ladder of his august career.
Scholars may well take issue with me here,
But it's my belief that, after four years,
He was back at Oxford as, it appears,
Professor of Astronomy! I mean,
Wren's brilliance verges on the obscene:

Rhyming History

Two chairs, in quite different disciplines,
And barely twenty-nine! Wren, for his sins,
Was loth to specialise. Why should he?
Nobody expected you to, you see,
Before the dead hand (as it seems to me)
Of the early twentieth century –
Or late nineteenth, perhaps. The days, sadly,
When a man could pursue soldiery,
Play at politics and write poetry,
Lecture now and then in astronomy
And (as did Wren) master anatomy
Are past. One of modern life's frustrations
Is the mad quest for qualifications,
Leading to narrow specialisations.
Expert in more than one field? Forget it.
Four strings to your bow? Sure to regret it.

Christopher Wren wins eternal respect
By changing tack and turning architect.

His first commission, no simple task,
Was from Gilbert Sheldon, who (since you ask)
Was called to the see of Canterbury,
As the new Archbishop, in '63.
The Sheldonian Theatre, so-called,
Was bold and unique. Critics were appalled.
Its roof was trussed timber! It was round-walled!
Daring and new, yet of classic design:
A target for every Philistine!

It's used to this day to confer degrees,
For university ceremonies,
For debates and plays (a rarity, these),
Even for music. The seats, if you please,
Are hard on the bum and tight on the knees.
But folk were much smaller in Christopher's day,
So lay off the architect, that's what I say.

Charles the Second and the Restoration

Formerly Warden of All Souls, Oxford
(From where he knew Wren), you can take my word
That Gilbert was, frankly, a tad absurd.
Building the Theatre made absolute sense,
Yet despite the fact that the massive expense
Was borne by himself (much to his credit),
Not once did he ever set foot in it!
Don't be put off, it's well worth a visit.
Those folk who know little or nothing of Wren,
After reading these lines, may well think again.

The rebuilding of London

Within days of the great conflagration
Wren tendered plans for the restoration
Of the City and, to give him his due,
His was a grand design. Evelyn, too,
Submitted a "plot for a new City".
Both men's far-reaching schemes, more's the pity,
Were rejected. Economic constraints
Dictated speed, and there were loud complaints
From those who feared that their property rights
Might be compromised, with unseemly fights
Over such issues as compensation.
To Christopher's obvious vexation,
There proved to be no splendid avenues,
No fine boulevards, no generous views.
Instead, the City was rebuilt piecemeal,
Unplanned, unfocused, with an *ad hoc* feel.
This was a rare, missed opportunity,
Bred of muddle and greed, and sad to see.

There were rules and regulations, however,
And here King Charles was undoubtedly clever.
Only buildings constructed of brick and stone
Were permitted, and this provision alone
Ensured that fire was a thing of the past
And that London's new structures were built to last.

Rhyming History

A new St. Paul's

Christopher Wren's outstanding legacy
Were his churches. There are still some to see.
St. James is a treasure (Piccadilly)
And another (restored painstakingly)
St. Stephen, in Walbrook (the best, for me).
Several were destroyed in World War Two,
I'm not sure how many (more than a few).
Some fifty churches, after the Fire,
Wren built (the number may have been higher).
But St. Paul's Cathedral, his work of art,
Is the finest by far. Where do I start?

The designs went through several stages.
The whole complex business took ages.
Wren's initial plans (in '69)
Were rejected as too 'foreign'. Well, fine –
But who knows? They might have been a great loss.
His next proposal was for a 'Greek Cross' –
With four arms (as it were) of equal length.
Sounds good to me. But Christopher's great strength
Was his persistence. When this was thrown out,
He embarked on a third design, without doubt
His favourite, the so-called 'Great Model'.
This proposal, as far as one can tell,
Was closer to what was finally built.
Charles backed it, we gather, up to the hilt.
Apparently Wren spent six hundred pounds
Just on the model (the figure astounds).
It's still in the crypt, to be seen today.

But the Dean and Chapter refused to pay
For this novel design (complete with Dome)
And rejected the plan. Poor Wren went home
And burst into tears, or so it's alleged.
Five years had been wasted. Christopher pledged

Charles the Second and the Restoration

To make no more models. One, however,
He did complete (with far less endeavour) –
And here he proved remarkably clever.
He served up the so-called 'Warrant Design',
His Dome topped by a tall, thin spire – sign,
He was sure, that this crass, compromise plan
Would find little favour. Wrong! To a man
(Chapter and Dean), they approved the new scheme!

So Wren set to work to pursue his dream.
A clause in his contract (subtle, you see)
Afforded the architect "liberty"
To make such changes "as from time to time
"He should see proper". And Wren (it's sublime)
Worked his magic. Behind the scaffolding
The Dean failed to see what was unfolding.
Serves him right, I say. To a large extent
Wren followed his 'Great Model'. The spire went,
The Dome now resplendent in all its glory –
The Dean, no doubt, incandescent with fury.

No words can render justice to St. Paul's.
Take your time, but when inspiration calls
Witness the wonder for yourself. The Dome –
Comparable to St. Peter's in Rome –
Is three hundred and sixty-five feet high.
Sorry to bang on. It's one reason why
St. Paul's is so famous. This will amaze:
Over sixty-five thousand tons it weighs.
In his old age (he died at ninety-one)
Wren would return to St. Paul's, his work done,
And sit under his great Dome, to reflect –
And offer up thanks to God, I suspect.

Christopher was a hands-on architect.
It was he who supervised the craftsmen,
Hired the stonemasons and carvers, often
From abroad. One such, commended to Wren,

Rhyming History

Was Grinling Gibbons, wood carver sublime.
John Evelyn, polymath of his time,
'Discovered' Gibbons "in a poor… thatched house"
In Holland. No craftsman could carve a mouse,
A leaf or a twig with such dexterity,
With such a "loose and airy lightness" as he.

Sir Christopher (as he became) would, weekly,
Inspect his creation from a basket. We,
Of course, now consider this curiously quaint.
But hauled up and down on a pulley? Safe, it ain't!

Many there were who feared that the great weight
Of the Dome would cause its collapse. Its fate
Became the subject of fevered debate.

On the day the scaffolding was removed,
Wren (the King would surely not have approved)
Watched the great unveiling from the high spot
Of Parliament Hill. Like it or not,

Should the Dome 'implode', he'd be gone that day
(His carriage was waiting), off and away!
Imagine: his reputation in tatters.
But St. Paul's stood the test. That's all that matters.

The Dutch raid on the Medway

Back to the plot. This was a dreadful time
For Charles. Was he (they whispered) past his prime?
Plague; fire; war: a grisly pantomime.
Revenues fell. Massive losses were made
In the wake of the fire – a slump in trade.
And the long Dutch war, as it trundled on,
Caused Charles to ask where his money had gone.
Conflicts are pricey, as simple as that,
And if this one differed, I'll eat my hat.

The Dutch, we're assured, were eager for peace –
Were anxious too for the stalemate to cease.
Yet they held the edge and Johann de Witt,
Of Holland, took full advantage of it.
In a stunning attack, a daring raid,
The Dutch sailed up the Medway. Unafraid
And ruthless, they blasted the English fleet,
Inflicting a comprehensive defeat:
An "incredible mischief" (Evelyn)
In a war that England could never win.

Many "of our best Men of War" were burnt.
If lessons were there to be learned, they weren't.
"Unaccountable negligence," John said,
For "lying at anchor". The King saw red,
Yet all he could do was to shake his head.
Evelyn, made of more resolute stuff,
Set out for Chatham. He wrote, off the cuff,
Of the "carcase" of the *London* (no joke),
"Now for the third time burnt", the *Royal Oak*
And the *James* to boot – all gone up in smoke,

Rhyming History

Indeed, "yet smoking". John called it (don't scoff)
"A dishonour never to be wiped off".
The *Royal Charles*, the vessel with pride of place
In the fleet, the Dutch towed away: disgrace,
Despair and dismay. De Witt played his ace.

These dark and troublesome events, great Heaven,
Occurred in the summer of '67.
By the Peace of Breda, in late July, **1667**
Hostilities ceased by agreement. Why,
You may ask, did it take such an age?
Stubbornness? Lassitude? Hard to gauge.
But trade was a factor, take it from me –
Commercial and nautical rivalry.

The Dutch, I regret, 'dabbled' in slavery.
There's just one word for that foul trade: knavery.
Confirmed (by Breda) in certain possessions
On the African coast, here their obsessions
With slaves (that most hideous exploitation)
Enjoyed free rein, to the shame of the nation.
The English (not unblemished, I have to say)
Held on to New York, which till King George's day,
The Third of that name, remained in our hands –
New Delaware also, one understands.
New Jersey too was awarded to us
Under Breda. Those who kicked up a fuss,
Protesting with passion the pact was bad,
Were wrong. These terms were the best to be had.
For England, sadly, was bankrupt and weak –
Badly in need of a break, so to speak…

Edward Hyde, Earl of Clarendon

…And a scapegoat. Poor Clarendon it was
Who was made to carry the can, because
(And only because) he was an old man,
Moral and upright, whose career began

Charles the Second and the Restoration

Long before most of the youngsters at Court
Had even been thought of. A noble sort,
Sober and proper, from another age,
The Earl was cruelly kicked off the stage.
Widely unpopular (not very fair),
He was portly, dull and lacking in flair.
Pompous (who cares?) and annoyingly 'right',
Clarendon, though, was undoubtedly bright.

Eclipsing every contemporary,
His record, in brief, was exemplary.
As Edward Hyde he had opposed the King –
Viz. Charles the First. To his way of thinking,
The royalist Court's contempt for the law
Was dangerous and damaging. Therefore,
In the early days he sided with Pym,
Standing shoulder to shoulder, backing him
In opposing the King's prerogative courts.

But before very long he had second thoughts.
Hyde was a moderate, Pym too extreme,
Responsible monarchy Edward's dream.
He believed in settlement, compromise
And peaceable terms. Charles, in his eyes,
Was England's divinely anointed King.
Nothing could deny his birthright, nothing.

Hyde declared for the King. What else could he do?
He pledged his allegiance – well, wouldn't you?
When hostilities opened in '42,
He stood by his side without further ado,
And that's where he stayed, dogged, loyal and true.

Charles' chief adviser during the war years,
Hyde never flinched, never faltered. Three cheers!
Faithful to the cause (for such was his style),
He followed the Crown Prince into exile.

Rhyming History

After the King's cruel execution,
Abhorring the so-called 'revolution',
He laboured hard for the one solution
To England's catastrophe: Restoration.

The new King was hardly Hyde's 'creation',
Yet Charles' return was of long gestation,
Well over a decade – eleven years
Of squabbles and factions, egos and tears,
Bred (I've no doubt) of subliminal fears
Of endless exile. It was Hyde alone
Who answered the call, who picked up the 'phone
(As it were) from the General, George Monck.
Jermyn and his cronies? In a blue funk!
Vermin and phonies, they hadn't a clue
(When offered the option) what they should do.

One man alone saved the day. That was Hyde,
The King's true counsellor, mentor and guide.
The Declaration of Breda was his –
He drafted it. A work of art it is!
All things to all men, it fitted the bill.
But now, poor chap, he was over the hill.

Hyde, it's fair to say, saved the monarchy
(That's quite some claim to fame) single-handedly.
Yet to Clarendon was shown no pity.
To boil it all down to the nitty-gritty,
They despised him: Barbara Castlemaine,
The King's mistress (and a right royal pain);
The Duke of Buckingham; the young brigade
At Court. For the Lord Chancellor was staid,
Solemn and puffed up. He wouldn't allow
His wife to receive the King's 'woman'. Well now,
This was unwise. But he refused to kowtow
To fashion and that's why they hated him.
They mocked the poor fellow, berated him,

Charles the Second and the Restoration

And sought his undoing. His daughter, Anne,
Had married James, Duke of York. Not his plan –
In fact, he opposed it. He was livid,
And sought to have her head chopped off, he did!
The very thought… I ask you, how obscene.
He never wished his daughter to be Queen,
Yet that, of course, was how it was perceived.
Clarendon denied it. Was he believed?
Of course not, no. But hey, that's politics –
A nest of rumour, bile and dirty tricks.

The Chancellor was also blamed (unfairly)
For Queen Catherine being barren. Scary!
He'd arranged the match, but hardly his fault,
I'd say, that she failed to 'breed'. This assault
Was short-lived. But the wretched man, perforce,
Was blamed for the Plague, the Fire (of course)
And that terrible raid on the Medway.

In foreign affairs, I do have to say,
His record (in the King's view anyway)
Was undistinguished. The fact that the French
Had joined with the Dutch (a most dreadful stench
This had occasioned) did little to quench
The flames now licking at Clarendon's feet.
Sickening, but the one man feeling the heat
Was the Chancellor. He was truly 'dead meat'
When Charles turned against him, his downfall complete.

The mob stoned his house in Piccadilly
And Parliament (this was plain silly)
Moved to impeach him. Here Charles drew the line.
Get rid of the duffer – yes, that was fine,
But impeachment? I mean… Resignation?
A far better course, by 'invitation'.
The King sent his brother, James, Duke of York
(The Earl's son-in-law), for a 'little talk'.

Rhyming History

But Clarendon declined (he'd nerves of steel)
To deliver the Chancellor's Great Seal,
Save to his sovereign. So, Fortune's wheel
Turned. The old Earl was sent for by the King
And dismissed – disgraceful and heart-rending.

A few days later, Evelyn (a friend)
Visited the ex-Chancellor and penned,
In his *Diary*, these words: "very sad"
He found him, "in his bed chamber". He had
"Enemies at Court… ladies of pleasure"
And "buffoons". He had taken their measure,
"Thwarted some of them and stood in their way".
Good for the old codger, that's what I say!
"Among the royal sufferers" (so-called)
"He made few friends." For many were appalled
That he "advanced the old rebels". Odd that –
But politic, surely. I'll eat my hat
Were it not sound policy. It was Hyde,
As he then was (and this can't be denied),
Who facilitated the King's return
To his inheritance. Men never learn,
But this was only achieved through compromise –
And unpopularity (surprise, surprise).

The former Chancellor, in Evelyn's eyes,
"Kept up the substance of things in the nation
"With more solemnity" (some reputation!)
"Than some would have had". John Evelyn's "kind friend"
He was "on all occasions". A sorry end.
"The Cabal prevailed" (we shall meet them anon)
And within a few weeks Clarendon was gone.

Into exile this honourable, old man went,
His ambition disappointed, his passion spent.
Parliament still passed an Act of Banishment –
Can you believe! What earthly harm could he do now?
Yet he outclassed them in his achievement, and how!

Charles the Second and the Restoration

As well as writing an autobiography,
He wrote (or rather completed) his *History*.
How he remembered it all is a mystery,
But his great *History of the Rebellion*
Was (and remains still) – sorry to go on and on –
The finest instance of historical writing
In the English language. I find that exciting.

After Clarendon

Every schoolboy's heard of the 'Cabal'.
All examination papers (banal)
Feature a mention of the 'Famous Five'.

The first letters of their surnames survive
As an acronym: C. A. B. A. L.
It helps the student remember them well.
'C' is for Clifford (zealous, a Catholic);
'A' is for Arlington (clever and quick);
'B' is for Buckingham (bright, but a cynic),
'A', Ashley-Cooper (a bit of a prick);
'L' is for Lauderdale (rough and bucolic,
Though not, as far as I know, alcoholic).

Rhyming History

When Clarendon fell, the Court was ecstatic.
But those who succeeded him… What made them tick?
They'd little in common, these chaps: secretive,
Strong-willed, watchful, canny and competitive.
They had no common policy. As I live,
This suited the King well. Divide and rule.
He used and abused them. Charles was no fool.
You should understand this from the outset –
The Cabal formed no kind of 'Cabinet'.

Clifford

Thomas, the 1st Lord Clifford, as we've seen,
Was a Catholic. He was more than keen
To promote the French interest. As such,
He was temperamentally anti-Dutch.
A *protégé* of Arlington, his rise
Was rapid and it comes as no surprise
That he was one of the covert parties
To a secret treaty which, if you please,
Charles signed in 1670 with France –
The 'first' Treaty of Dover. At first glance,
This seemed like utter madness, and it was.
The Treaty was made in secret because
Charles agreed to become a Catholic!
Why? I haven't a clue. It's fantastic.

Clifford was important as an ally
To the King in this process, and here's why.
He served as a Member of Parliament
And lobbied on behalf of the government
In the Commons, a Court spokesman, as it were –
Though he kept mum about France, without demur.

Arlington

Arlington, Clifford's senior by twelve years,
Likewise was privy (so at least it appears)

Charles the Second and the Restoration

To the Treaty of Dover (the secret one).
A shabby character when all's said and done,
He never was popular. Stiff and formal,
He sported a patch on his nose (not normal) –
An old war wound, he claimed. Buckingham loathed him.
Arlington was slippery and a bit prim.
Hardworking (but shifty), he had served the King
For long years in exile, doggedly winning
The royal favour. Come the Restoration,
He secured for himself a situation
In charge (in effect) of foreign policy,
In which post he was lucky, it seems to me,
To survive at all. The Dutch War went badly;
The Treaty of Breda proved a dud, sadly.
Many there were who'd have strangled him, gladly.

Yet they let old Clarendon carry the can,
A monster injustice (but then I'm a fan).
Arlington, rather, was surely their man.

Buckingham

The Duke of Buckingham had been brought up
With Charles as a boy. An arrogant pup,
He was good-looking (like his father), bright,
Witty, personable and (if I'm right)
A musician and a fine playwright.
He squandered these talents, for he was vain,
Wayward and vicious. It's hard to explain
His uncanny talent for survival.
The Earl of Shrewsbury was a rival –
The Countess was the Duke's mistress. So what?
Buckingham took advantage. A poor shot
Was the Earl. So the mad Duke murdered him –
Just like that! In a duel! On a whim!
Charles pardoned the villain. Crazy or what?
But the Duke was excused, like it or not.

Rhyming History

A firm favourite with the 'easy' King,
His influence was simply sickening.
For Buckingham (this bit gives me the creeps)
Was said to "rule all", according to Pepys.
He hated Clarendon, surely jealous.
For where the poor Chancellor was zealous,
Upright, gifted, honest and diligent,
Buckingham lacked morals, was indigent,
Untrustworthy, shifty and negligent.

Yet, as early as 1662,
The King appointed him (what can you do?)
To the Privy Council. Clarendon, true,
Stemmed the Duke's influence during his 'reign',
But the old Earl's fall was Buckingham's gain.
The King sent his friend on missions abroad,
Though I hear the Duke was often ignored.
He was led to believe (I do like this)
That the (second) Treaty of Dover was 'his' –
The one that didn't matter, the one, that is,
That kept the Catholic clauses hidden.
Arlington knew, but he was forbidden
(Along with Clifford) to disclose the truth.
No wonder that Buckingham loathed them. Strewth!
Some Cabal! Subterfuge, truculence, infighting…
The King must have found it all rather exciting!

The Duke, we shall see, came to a sad end.
For he set himself up (Heaven forfend!)
As a Protestant champion. Well now,
Buckingham got his come-uppance, and how!
His hypocrisy was stomach-churning.
Simultaneously he was 'earning'
(Useful word) backhanders from the French King,
Louis the Fourteenth, that arch-Catholic.
I don't claim to know what made Buckingham tick,
But his nerve was breathtaking and makes me sick.

Charles the Second and the Restoration

Ashley Cooper

Anthony Ashley Cooper, a rum cove,
Was a perfidious turncoat. By Jove!
I've quite lost count of the number of times
This blackguard changed sides. I've run out of rhymes!

In the early years of the Civil War
He fought for the King. But in '44,
All of a rush, he was for Parliament.
Was this simply a matter of discontent
With the royalist cause or, as I suspect,
The knack of sniffing a winner? Circumspect,
Selfish and cool (an ugly combination),
The sole object of Ashley's admiration
Was himself. He sat on the Council of State
During the Commonwealth, but there's some debate
As to his true opinion of Cromwell.
They must have got on, as far as one can tell,
In the first promise of the Protectorate.
But Ashley soon fell out with Ollie, you bet!

That's the pattern. At first all sweetness and light –
Then the growl, the bark and finally the bite.

Never quite in step with Cromwell, no surprise,
Therefore, that after the Protector's demise
He cast his eye abroad. There was no knowing
How long Charles might last. But the breeze was blowing
From the Continent. So he sided with Monck.
Bring the King home! The Protectorate was sunk.

Promotion was swift. Lord Ashley he became,
As skilfully, subtly, he made his name.
Yet he knew his own mind. The Clarendon Code
He opposed, the first step on a rocky road

Rhyming History

Of increasing confrontation with the King.
Yet Charles was ever canny. If anything,
It suited him to have Lord Ashley on side.
Indeed, the King took his Lordship for a ride
Over Dover. Like Buckingham, he kept him
Well and truly in the dark. Though far from dim,
Poor Ashley hadn't the remotest idea
Of the Treaty's Catholic clauses – oh, dear!

Still, he won high office. In '72
He became Lord Chancellor; and an Earl, too –
The Earl of Shaftesbury. All perfectly true.
Yet he was soon at odds (this was nothing new)
With the King. He backed the infamous Test Act –
A stubborn and foolhardy course, that's a fact.
His independence of spirit, nonetheless,
Earned him praise in some quarters, that I confess.
Yet he fell from grace and I couldn't care less.

Charles saw through Shaftesbury. 'Little Sincerity'
He called him – whether meanly or merrily,
I know not. You may say I'm being too hard.
Indeed, it's impossible to disregard
His support for the King's two Declarations
Of Indulgence. The breakdown in relations,
Though (really quite nasty), still came about
Over religion, of that there's no doubt.

The King's flirtation with Catholicism,
And with France, led to hostility, schism,
Unease and suspicion. I'm running ahead –
Test Acts and the like – but it has to be said
That Shaftesbury was a seminal figure,
A man of huge intellectual rigour.
How the ass threw it all away we shall see.
A sad and terrible waste it seems to me.

Charles the Second and the Restoration

Lauderdale

Of the famous Cabal, the fifth member
Is one whom students seldom remember.
'L' is for Lauderdale, the 2nd Earl
(And the 1st Duke). I could make your toes curl
With tales of Lauderdale's unscrupulous
Doings. Some Scots kicked up a rare old fuss
When the King, upon his Restoration,
Impressed by Lauderdale's reputation,
Appointed him Secretary of State –
For Scotland, that is. I'm telling you straight,
Lauderdale was an unappealing chap.
Coarse, brutish and crude, he loved a good scrap.
As a Presbyterian he was opposed
To Charles the First, so it might have been supposed
That he'd make the most unlikely candidate
To govern Scotland for his son. Well, that's Fate.

For in '47 he decided
To change his allegiance and sided
With old King Charles. The so-called 'Engagement'
Was concluded, by which strange arrangement
The Scots were to restore Charles to his throne,
By force. In return, so far as is known,
For Lauderdale's sworn pledge (he gave his word)
Charles would establish (naïve and absurd)
Presbyterianism, within three years,
South of the border. Bound to end in tears,
And it did. In the second Civil War –
The King's responsibility, for sure –
The Scottish army, its collapse complete,
Went down at Preston to massive defeat.
Lauderdale, though (it's high time I said it),
Was fiercely loyal (much to his credit)
To the Stuart cause. Earlier that year
It was he, quite openly, without fear,

Rhyming History

Who offered succour and sanctuary
To the Prince of Wales. Charles actually
Liked Lauderdale. When, in 1650,
As King, he sailed to Scotland, finally,
He warmed to the old rogue – apparently
The only Scot he could stand! When, at Scone,
Charles was crowned King (not a moment too soon),
This honest man was vocal in support
Of his sovereign. His service, in short,
Was exemplary. He fought for the King
At Worcester. Loyalty: Lauderdale's thing!

He, the Duke of Buckingham, and Derby
Escaped with the King, though, regrettably,
He was waylaid and lost his liberty,
Spending nine long years in captivity.
Buckingham was caught, but escaped to France.
Derby, however, got no second chance.
Less fortunate than Lauderdale, poor chap,
He was an Englishman, so took the rap –
Execution. Lauderdale was excused:
A Scot, he knew no better! Aren't you amused?

Come the Restoration, it's no surprise
That Lauderdale prospered. His hard-earned rise
Was Scotland's gain – well, according to some.
Others, quite frankly, were less overcome.
For the simple truth is that Lauderdale
Was ruthless, dogged, and fought tooth and nail
In the King's interest. Charles was content
To leave things to his 'viceroy', if this meant
An easeful life. And so it was to prove.

For the Scots always stood at one remove
From the King's heart. You may recall the days
When the Covenanters forced their weird ways
On the young King. This was more than a phase.

Charles the Second and the Restoration

The Presbyterians were ever keen
To press their influence. Now, call me green,
But Charles, I'd say, harboured deep resentment
At the way he'd been treated. Discontent,
Boredom, frustration – call it what you will;
But the Scots and their faith? A bitter pill.
Presbyterians were persecuted
Under Lauderdale. Sadly, this suited
The lazy English King, who couldn't care less
If a few Scottish zealots suffered distress.

Lauderdale governed, you can bet your life,
With an iron fist. Corruption was rife;
Nepotism, too. His troublesome wife,
Flame-haired and brash, with a tongue like a knife,
Added colour and scandal, sugar and spice,
And at bottom, I gather, wasn't that nice.

The Triple Alliance   1668

Foreign affairs fast became a quagmire
Following Clarendon's fall. I admire
Charles' nerve, one has to, but the next five years
(A humble estimate) gave rise to fears
(Nay, accusations) of duplicity,
Bad faith, corruption and conspiracy.
Harsh words, but his *chutzpah* was amazing.
He fibbed for England; simply hair-raising.

By January 1668
Charles showed himself keen to negotiate
A far more lasting accord with the Dutch.
He hadn't much time for Holland, as such,
But Parliament liked the sound of it.
The Dutch were Protestants, you see. De Witt
(Whom we've met) first proposed the alliance
In order, I've read, to isolate France.
Sweden joined in this diplomatic dance,

113

Rhyming History

And so the Triple Alliance was born.
The Treaty, of course, was greeted with scorn
By the likes of Clifford (a Catholic,
Cautious, pro-French, and a crusty old stick),
But the King gave his blessing. Why, you ask?
I'll try to explain (an arduous task).
He loathed the Dutch. Remember the Medway?
The King, though, was broke. At the end of the day,
Poor Charles was dependent for his livelihood
On supply from the Commons. So far, so good.

The Dutch feared the French. They were scared stiff in fact.
The latter were brutal and lacking in tact.
Their forces had recently overrun
The Spanish Netherlands, hardly much fun.
The United Provinces, they'd be next.
The Dutch were frightened; the Spanish were vexed;
And the English… ? That remains to be seen,
Though De Witt, I'm sure, was fatally green
In trusting our King. I'd call it obscene,

Were I a Dutchman. I've more than a hunch
That Charles and his cronies (a fickle bunch:
Clifford and Arlington the main players)
Saw this as the first of many layers
In a strategy to woo France. How come?

Well, though it may not appear so to some,
Louis the Fourteenth of France wasn't dumb.
Far from it! He now felt out on a limb,
And fear of loneliness wasn't for him.
Nor was his cousin in England so dim:
An alliance or nothing! Sink or swim!

Secret deals

Within months of the Triple Alliance
Charles (acting, as it were, in defiance
Of the agreement) responded, with glee,
To an approach by his cousin Louis –
Shrouded in the greatest secrecy –
To forge a new alliance of their own!

The King was lucky to have kept his throne,
Given the high level of recklessness
Involved in this strategy. I confess
To remaining completely in the dark
As to his motives. The dangers were stark,
Potent and immediate. Charles agreed
Readily with Lou on the pressing need
(Allow me to quote) to "humble the pride"
Of the Dutch by joining his cousin's side
Against the United Provinces. And,
Believe this, upward of two hundred grand
(A significant sum) was to be paid
To Charles by Louis. The Commons were dismayed –
Or would have been had they known about it!
For this demonstrated how, bit by bit,

Rhyming History

Charles was holding Parliament in contempt.
From the odd subterfuge no King is exempt,
But this bare-faced arrogance took the biscuit.

Heaven knows how Charles was prepared to risk it,
But even while planning this new alliance
He was seeking fresh funds to wage war on France –
From the Commons! Yet what appears at first glance
To have been a tricky Treaty looks far worse
Upon closer analysis. Risk-averse?
Charles? I don't think so! For there was one more clause
In the French agreement… Now, take a wee pause…
A deep breath… I do believe you'll need it. The King
Declared in the Treaty – this, more than anything,
Astonishes – that he was "convinced of the truth
"Of the Roman Catholic religion". Strewth!

Had this strange admission ever got out
There'd have been Civil War, without any doubt.
Under the terms of the Treaty, nonetheless,
Charles was pledged to announce (bonkers, I confess)
His ready conversion to the Church of Rome:
Popular in France, fine; hardly so at home!
No particular timetable was imposed
For this 'revelation'. It must be supposed
That the terms were left deliberately vague.

Charles avoided this commitment like the plague.
He never declared himself a Catholic.
So why make the pledge? Who knows what made him tick?
Not I; nor any historians I've read.
The most compelling view, it has to be said,
Is that Charles the Second, a born romantic,
So admired his first cousin (a Catholic)
That he sought to demonstrate his close kinship
In the form of a 'special relationship'.

Charles the Second and the Restoration

Your guess is as good as mine. It's a mystery –
The best in seventeenth century history.

Charles was no fool. The clause was dynamite.
The secret Treaty was kept watertight.
On the English side Thomas Clifford knew,
And Arlington. Indeed, only a few
Were enlightened as to the deal at all.
Buckingham thought that he was walking tall
When asked to negotiate, on his own
(You know what they say: "Give a dog a bone…"),
The very same Treaty, but missing out
The Catholic clause! No shadow of doubt,
Charles was laughing all the way to the bank.

'Minette'

He had Princess Henriette-Anne to thank,
His adored little sister, for her part
In facilitating the pact. Her heart,
Her life, her soul were her brother's. 'Minette',
The King called her, his beloved, his pet.
She was fourteen years his junior and yet
Their bond was deep-rooted and immutable.
Minette was pretty, rather than beautiful –
Sweet-tempered and delicate. Every day
She and Charles exchanged letters, such was their way.

Yet Minette was unhappy, I'm sad to say,
For her husband was spiteful, jealous (and gay).
The Duc d'Orléans was brother to Louis,
Thus placing his young wife, well nigh perfectly,
As the ideal intermediary
Between Charles and the French King. Diplomacy
Was thus kept squarely within the family!
Under cover of the utmost secrecy –

Conditions which suited the English King fine –
The negotiations, throughout '69,   **1669**
Proceeded apace. Discussions were delayed
By the dreadful Duc, who was frankly dismayed
At the thought of his wife travelling abroad.
He was quick to quarrel and easily bored,
But the following year he gave his consent.

Minette's arrival was a wondrous event.   **1670**
No sooner had she borne the passage over
Than Charles signed the secret Treaty of Dover.
She'd brought it with her! It's hotly debated
How much of the deal was negotiated
By Minette herself. But she deserves applause
(From those so inclined) for the Catholic clause.
Indeed, she might have been the very reason
For its inclusion. Secrets were in season,
For Death, it appears, held his mysteries too.

Minette's visit caused a great hullabaloo –
Celebrations, feasting… For Charles' birthday
His fortieth, fell during his sister's stay.
His joy was at its zenith. But, lackaday,
Within weeks his fragile, cherished Minette lay dead.
She suffered awful agonies on her deathbed,
Peritonitis the cause, pain beyond belief.
When the King heard the news, he was stricken with grief.

Two Treaties

Still, on the 22nd of May Charles signed
The secret Treaty. Arlington was resigned,
Though not keen; Clifford was enthusiastic.
The second Treaty (I find this fantastic)
Was signed on the 21st of December –
By the entire Cabal. Pray remember,

Though, that Ashley, Buckingham and Lauderdale
Were in ignorance of the first! Without fail,
You'd think, the King was on course for disaster.
In the art of deceit, though, Charles was a master.

The most astonishing factor, to my mind,
Is that Parliament was totally blind
To both treaties! Fight the perfidious Dutch?
Our allies, surely… Not that Charles cared that much
What the Commons felt (or Lords, for that matter).
Charles, I submit, was as mad as a hatter
To leave his Parliament out on a limb.
The likes of consultation were not for him.
On he ploughed and merrily won supply
From the Commons (he barely had to try)
To strengthen his Navy against the threat
Of the French *and* the Dutch. Cheeky? You bet.
Despite these funds, Charles needed more money.
This would be sad if it weren't so funny,
But, still distrustful of Parliament,
He enlarged his standing Army. This meant,
Could only mean, that he feared a showdown.

Absolute power

In Scotland Lauderdale (that noble clown)   **1671**
Enlisted over 20,000 men
In the King's interest. What of that, then?
This sudden armed force was obliged to go
Anywhere, any time, on the say-so
Of the King. Parliament, you should know,
Stood prorogued, not in session at the time.
Nevertheless, this royal pantomime
Failed to impress. Is it any surprise
They felt threatened? They could only surmise
That the King had a vested interest
In feathering afresh the royal nest.

Rhyming History

Charles' strategy was injudicious.
Folk were increasingly suspicious
Of a drift towards absolute power.

Apprehension mounted by the hour,
Not least when Charles took the "false step" (his phrase)
Of a "Stop on the Exchequer". These days,
No one expects the Queen to have to raise
Her own finance to prosecute a war.
Patently that's what governments are for.
But Charles needed cash for his Dutch campaign:
He hadn't a bean (a constant refrain).
The Stop on the Exchequer took the strain.
In a nutshell, loans ceased to be repaid
In their due sequence. Lenders felt betrayed
As their credit collapsed. Bankers, dismayed
At Charles' apparent contempt for the rules,
Stopped lending altogether. They weren't fools!
Nobody likes seeing their hard-earned cash
Misappropriated. The 'Stop' was rash,
Ill considered and counterproductive.

Yet the logic must have proved seductive.
The 'Stop' rendered the King independent,
At least for a time, of Parliament.
The quite unprecedented discontent
That this aroused, though, caused permanent harm.
A figure of warmth and personal charm,
Was the King, they whispered, losing his touch?

A new Declaration of Indulgence

The price to be paid for war with the Dutch
Proved, when it came to the crunch, decisive.
However, the war was less divisive
Than the measure which (by a mere few days)
Preceded it. This, I'm sure, will amaze,

But Charles announced (it makes no kind of sense)
A new Declaration of Indulgence –
In the middle of March, '72.   **1672**
You'd think he might have waited, wouldn't you,
For the Lords and Commons to approve the war
Before making his move. They gave him what for.

The King sought to bypass Parliament
In the matter. He claimed that their consent
To the Declaration was not needed.
Their furious protests went unheeded,
Until, of course, he was short of money
For battle. He found it far from funny
When the Commons refused to countenance
His proposed reform. A new alliance
With the French against the Dutch was one thing,
But these hostilities were as nothing
Against the dangers of a fickle King
Hell-bent on claiming (this was sickening)
An inherent power ("supreme," he said)
In religious affairs. The blockhead!

Any surprise that the Commons saw red?
The Cavalier Parliament, so-called,
Was anti-Catholic. They were appalled
At the catastrophic implications
Of the Declaration. Indications
Of their disgust became ever more clear
When they passed into law (revenge, I fear)
The dreaded Test Act the following year.
This terrible statute raised half a cheer,
Even from Protestant zealots – oh, dear!

We'll return to the Test Acts later. I'm aware
That certain readers may be driven to despair
By all this talk of war and of Declarations,
Of treaties with France, and worsening relations

Rhyming History

Between the King and his angry Parliament.
I'm sorry. It was never my professed intent
To get bogged down in politics. I've had enough
(And so have you, I'd hazard) of this boring stuff.
Charles the Second, we're told, had many a mistress.
I've consulted the authorities and it's this,
His love life, that I've decided to turn to now.
For the King was a veritable rogue, I vow!

The King's mistresses

There were dozens of women in Charles' life –
Hundreds, who knows? There was only one wife.
Catherine of Braganza, as we've seen,
Was his long-suffering and loyal Queen.
She was forced to accept (and this she did)
A whole string of mistresses: sad, sordid

And cruel. In this she had little choice.
Had she once raised her mild, Portuguese voice
Against her husband's sexual excess,
She'd have kissed goodbye to his sweet caress.
For they shared a bed, that can't be denied,
And they tried for children – oh, how they tried!

Lucy Walter

The first mistress of any relevance
Was Lucy Walter. Her significance
Became apparent many years later
When Charles' son James, a smooth operator,
Claimed (his rash supporters did anyway)
Legitimate status. As was his way,
Charles was quite relaxed about the whole thing.
He acknowledged the brat, but (here's the sting)
He denied (was forced to deny, in fact)
Marriage to Miss Walter. Lucy lacked tact.
She took other lovers, went to the bad,
And at times appeared to be raving mad –
For example, when she sought custody
Of the boy. The matter of bastardy
Apart, the King doted on his wee child
And asserted his right. Lucy went wild,
Shouting and screaming in the street, we're told,
Like a crazed banshee or a common scold.

The poor girl has my sympathy. She died,
Young, of venereal disease. She tried,
Hard, to be a good mother. John Evelyn
Called her "insipid". Since when was that a sin?

Charles was still in his twenties when Lucy
Caught his idle fancy. Exile, you see,
Gave ample room for affairs of the heart,
Amorous adventures, where Cupid's dart

Pierced many a ready, receptive breast.
Born under Venus, the King did his best
To rise to the challenge – and rise he did.
There's no need for rudeness, Heaven forbid,
But Charles (it's alleged) was hung like a horse.
Sorry, I did promise not to get coarse,
But I've said it, there – so what can you do?
It's out! Don't get yourselves into a stew.
No naughtier, truly, I have to say
Than the ditties and rhymes of Charles' own day,
Which praised his potency, sang of his strength,
Commending, too, his "prodigious length".
His "sceptre" was… No, perhaps enough said –
My readers, I'm sure, are far too well bred.

Barbara Palmer

Barbara Palmer was voluptuous,
Beauteous, lewd and avaricious.
She could also, in truth, be vicious,
Temperamental and – wonderful word –
Ravenous. Pepys (why does this sound absurd?)
"Glutted" himself with looking on her face,
Even dreamt of being in her embrace,
And he a civil servant! A disgrace!

There was most certainly no denying
Barbara's charms. Accomplished at crying,
She could at times be mightily trying.
Charles wasn't good at putting up with fits
And temper tantrums. Babs had high spirits,
A warm heart, a cool brain and nerves of steel.
Above all, she had awesome sex appeal.
Her willowy figure, rich auburn hair
And wistful blue eyes drove men to despair.
She was the King's mistress for seven years,
Enjoying royal favour, it appears,

Charles the Second and the Restoration

From shortly before his Restoration.
Palmer was her married name. The nation
Was faintly scandalised (or so we're told)
That a youthful monarch could be so bold
As to sleep with another fellow's wife.
Poor Roger Palmer! It cut like a knife
To be cuckolded by his own sovereign.
Charles, admittedly, wasn't living in sin.
Catherine, his loving Queen, was yet to come,
Though he led her a merry dance, and then some!

As for Barbara, she drove the King insane.
He was mad for love. The Earl of Castlemaine
Roger became, a sop to his pride, I'd say.
Her bloom faded fast (that's Nature's cruel way).
By the time the Countess had outlived her stay
She'd borne the King five children (with some debate
Re. a sixth – denied by Charles, at any rate).

We've seen how the unfortunate Catherine
Gave way to defeat, a war she'd never win.
Whichever of the King's mistresses was 'in',
She was obliged to show courtesy, respect
And resignation. What else did she expect,
A barren disappointment from Portugal,
But distant contempt? Charles even had the gall,
As we've read, to foist the dreadful Barbara
On the Queen as lady-in-waiting. A star,
Catherine behaved with consummate dignity
And accepted her fate. Well done, your Majesty.

Women never influenced policy.
His last mistress's catholicity –
We'll come to her later, so you can see –
Gave rise to suspicions that the King
Was doing more at night than listening
To idle pillow talk, and discussing

Affairs of state with those whom he shouldn't.
All I can say is, Charles simply wouldn't.
He knew his own mind. Women were his friends,
As well as serving his sexual ends.
He enjoyed their company, liked to chat,
Laugh and be entertained – but that was that.

Nell Gwynn

Entertainment, of course, was the *forte*
Of Nelly Gwynn. Nell was very naughty,
Sexy and impish, a breath of fresh air.
Castlemaine, sadly, could only despair.
Too old at twenty-nine, she was outshone,
Outclassed and outwitted. Her looks were gone
And Charles lost interest. "Make the least noise
"You can," he demanded. Women were toys,
You may take from that – and Kings, little boys.

"Pretty, witty Nell" (as described by Pepys:
The middle-aged lech, he gives me the creeps)

Charles the Second and the Restoration

Was on the stage by the age of fourteen.
A "bold, merry slut" she may well have been
(Pepys again, can you believe?), she was ace
In comedy. Not just a pretty face,
She had perfect legs and delicate feet,
Was impertinent, wild and indiscreet.

The King was enraptured. They chanced to meet
In the dying days of Barbara's reign,
Confirming the end of old Castlemaine.
Nelly was seventeen (eighteen at most).
Her earlier lovers, she liked to boast,
Embraced two more Charleses. So 'Charles the Third'
The King became! She was saucy, my word!

She coined other wonderful nicknames too –
James, Duke of York: 'Dismal Jimmy'. She knew
That Charles wouldn't mind. He laughed like a drain,
Returning for more again and again.
One rival, Louise de Kéroualle, asked why
She was dubbed 'Squintabella'. Nell was sly:
Sadly, Louise had a cast in one eye.
Like Barbara P, Lou liked a good cry
(That is, she threw temper tantrums) and so
She became, for her pains, 'Weeping Willow'!

This may be something you'd rather not know,
But Nell and Louise enjoyed Charles' favours
For many a year, right royal ravers!
Both were survivors and shared the King's bed –
Never together, it has to be said –
Till his dying day. Nell was Protestant;
Louise, Catholic. You get what you want
In this life and Nell, she fought tooth and nail
To feather her nest. Oh, how she did rail
Against all the privileges enjoyed
By Babs and Louise. She was that annoyed!

Rhyming History

The former became Duchess of Cleveland;
The latter, Duchess of Portsmouth: so grand!
Poor Nell couldn't readily understand
How she was ignored. Down to class, of course.
An orange seller could yell herself hoarse
Before winning a title. One success,
Though, Nell did enjoy. She couldn't care less
(When it came to the crunch) for her own worth,
Proud as she was of her nondescript birth.
But she struggled to comprehend how on earth
The King could omit to honour their son.

So one day, in front of everyone,
Her offspring she called "little bastard". "Why,"
Asked Charles, "do you insult the boy so?" "Fie!"
Replied Nell, "What fitter form of address
"Does he merit?" With no hint of bitterness,
The King conferred a dukedom on the young lad,
Then and there, proving there never was to be had
A fairer, more honest or more generous dad.

Nelly's wit and sense of humour were priceless.
Not necessarily renowned for 'niceness',
She was famous for her ready repartee.
The mob occasioned her some anxiety
At Oxford, mistaking Miss Gwynn for Louise.
They jostled her coach, attacking, if you please,
The bitch they declared to be Charles' Catholic
Harlot. Such naked prejudice makes me sick,
But, ever in high spirits, Nell saved the day.
Sticking her head out of the coach window, "Pray!"
She cried, "Good people, be civil!" (this I adore –
So witty, so sharp) "I am the Protestant whore!"

Though never destined for the giddy heights
Of Lou or Babs, Nell asserted her 'rights'.
Poor she was not! Mistresses, on the whole,
Relished their place on the royal payroll.

Nelly, I've read, had a pad in the Mall,
A coach, six horses, and servants withal.
An income of several thousand pounds,
Per annum, was hers. The figure astounds.
For a poor illiterate (Welsh to boot),
That wasn't half bad. But Nelly was cute,
Outspoken, ambitious, tough and astute.

Countess of Greenwich she would have become –
Attractive enough, though hardly a plum –
Had Charles not perished before the event.
He cried on his deathbed (ever the gent),
"Let not poor Nelly starve!" Who'd have placed bets
That 'Dismal Jimmy' would settle her debts?
Yet he did, astounding everyone
By granting Nell and her surviving son
A country estate! When all's said and done,

Rhyming History

King James was a generous kind of chap.
A shame he brought mishap after mishap
Down upon his head. I'm running ahead,
But James was a brick, it has to be said.

One of Nell's two sons (with Charles) died aged nine.
Herself, she suffered a sudden decline,
Struck down by a stroke at thirty-seven.
Whether or not she fetched up in Heaven
We can't be sure. It's not easy to tell.
She'd have bidden her Charles a sad farewell,
Had God in his wisdom sent her to hell.

Other mistresses

The King had no shame. Women came and went.
Though not as low (quite) as Nelly's 'descent',
There was Moll Davis, another actress,
Who nonetheless proved a short-lived success.
She bore Charles a daughter, a pretty child
Named Mary Tudor, sweet-tempered and mild,
Who in later life achieved noble rank.
For Moll's dismissal we've Nell Gwynn to thank.
For rumour has it (it's probably true:
'Foul play' by our Nellie was nothing new)
That she prepared a secret laxative
For Moll (amusing, though hard to forgive)
Before she 'dined' with the King. As I live,
This was underhand and shabby indeed.
The strategy, though, was set to succeed.
Poor Moll unexpectedly fell from grace,
And Nell stepped up smartly to take her place.

Briefly, too, there was one Winifred Wells,
A goddess-like figure, so legend tells.
Some found her character rather obtuse.
Barbara thought she resembled a goose;

Charles the Second and the Restoration

A "dreamy sheep," said another (that's strong).
Winifred sadly, though, didn't last long.
There was then Mrs. Knight, a fleeting choice,
Renowned for her "incomparable" voice –
That's Evelyn again. The list goes on.
Elizabeth Killigrew was outshone
By Catherine Pegge. Both bore Charles offspring
(Killigrew, one; Pegge, two), born to the King
In exile. He fathered in all (for sure)
Thirteen royal bastards, probably more.

Charles doted on his children, though the first,
His favourite, was most surely the worst.
James, Duke of Monmouth, was certainly cursed.
He died a shameful death at thirty-six,
A victim of his own histrionics,
Vanity, pride and dodgy politics.

Louise de Kéroualle

Back to the King's women! The fair Louise
Was pretty and plump and eager to please.
Some even thought her a bit of a tease.
But you hardly have to be Socrates
To explain her unpopularity.
For Lou was Catholic and French, you see –
Louise de Kéroualle. Some folk couldn't
Pronounce her name (or rather they wouldn't).
'Madame Carewell' she became. As for Nell,
Louise turned her nose up, like a bad smell.
A snob she was, as vain and as haughty
As Nell was lowly, common and naughty.

Evelyn didn't mince his words: a whore
He thought her, a "concubine". Furthermore,
"Prostitute creatures" he dubbed Portsmouth, Nell
And Cleveland, all three. He balked at 'Carewell':

Rhyming History

'Quirreval' she was when she first arrived
In Minette's train of ladies (quite contrived),
Then 'Quierovil'. I've noticed Evelyn,
Throughout his *Diary* (hardly a sin),
Employs different spellings all the time.
I couldn't care less, provided they rhyme.

As I've hinted, Louise first met the King
When Charles was busy negotiating
The (secret) Treaty of Dover. Minette
Took her duties seriously, you bet,
And refused to admit the young virgin
Into Charles' clutches. The King, in a spin,
Fell for the damsel hook, line and sinker.
Now Charles could be a bit of a stinker
(This we know), but Minette was insistent.

After her death Lou was less resistant.
Buckingham (himself a bit of a cad)
'Arranged' her passage over from France. Sad
For *la belle fille*, traded like a chattel.
Girls were treated like so many cattle.
But the sad, unfortunate lass was poor –
Penniless, in fact, and she knew the score.

The King's new mistress she quickly became,
Achieving, as such, wealth, prestige and fame.
When Evelyn first saw her (in her place
As Minette's lady, before her 'disgrace'),
He noted her "simple and baby face".
Already a "famed beauty", nonetheless
He considered her "childish". I confess
That John, for once, hadn't got it quite right.
Louise was no child. Formidably bright,
She well knew how to look out for herself,
And contrived to accumulate vast wealth.

Charles the Second and the Restoration

Evelyn was "casually showed" one day
Her "apartment at Whitehall". Blown away,
As he was, he recorded in detail
The "richness and glory" on a fine scale –
"Ten times… beyond the Queen's". Some indictment!
For her comfort and her entertainment,
Lou's accommodation was refurbished
(Nay, "rebuilt") three times, lavishly furnished
With "pendule clocks… tables… screens", what-have-you,
"French tapestry" of enormous value,
"Many pieces of plate… sconces… and stands" –
John's sense of wonderment one understands –
And the "best paintings", easy on the eye,
The like not seen before outside Versailles!
If anyone should ever ask you why
Louise was loathed, you now know your reply.

She was booed at the theatre – what sauce!
There was even one attempt (quashed, of course)
To try her as a common prostitute.
But Charles loved his Louise. She was a beaut,
Buxom (just the wrong side of curvaceous),
Alluring, intelligent, vivacious
And fun. Her critics dubbed her rapacious.
She did enjoy a huge annuity,
Some ten thousand pounds. For the King, you see,
Was smitten by his 'Fubbs', as he called her.
Though the Protestants (and Nell) stone-walled her,
Louise, for all her tantrums, tricks and tears,
Was a boon companion in the years
Of Charles' decline (if you can call them that).

For as time rolled on he enjoyed a chat,
A cosy, comfortable habitat –
And a good supper, it has to be said.
It's even rumoured he took to his bed

Rhyming History

To sleep (on the odd occasion, at least).
It wasn't a case of famine or feast –
Oh, no. For Louise, and even the Queen,
And Nelly for sure (I have to come clean)
Kept him snug in bed (you know what I mean).
They indulged old Charles till his dying day.
Lucky for some, I am tempted to say.

These three women were with him at the end.
Nelly had hysterics. Heaven forfend!
Queen Catherine begged his forgiveness – sad,
Given the terrible time that she'd had.
Louise kept her head. She helped find the priest
Who heard the King's confession. So, at least,
Charles died a Catholic. Such was his will,
We are led to believe. A bitter pill
For those Protestants to swallow. But Lou,
Smart to the end, ensured they never knew.
Some were suspicious, but what could they do?

The debauched Court raised many an eyebrow.
Evelyn records ('holier than thou')
A visit, just days before Charles' demise,
To the royal bedchamber. His old eyes
Were on stalks! The King was "in his undress".
John would never forget "the profaneness,
"Gaming" and the "total forgetfulness
"Of God" – for this was on a Sunday night.
Evelyn, indeed, had a rare old fright,
Witness to the King "sitting and toying
"With his concubines" (no shame), enjoying
"A French boy singing love songs", destroying
Any sense of decent regality.
This was "a scene of utmost vanity".
"Great courtiers", described as "dissolute",
Were at cards. John's horror was absolute:
"A bank of at least 2000 in gold"
Was in play. Call him a spoilsport, a scold,

But here was luxury on a grand scale
And Evelyn was there to tell the tale.
The party had to end. He knew it must.
For "six days after was all in the dust".

These hints at the King's death are premature.
Charles had years yet to live, at least twelve more.
We'd only reached 1673
Before (a little incongruously)
I broke off to speak of the business
Of his sex life, his taste in mistresses.

It's worth noting, though, before we wind back,
How, to the end, he never lost the knack
Of squeezing every last ounce out of life.
Ostensibly blind to the care and strife
Of state affairs, he displayed a fine flair
For living. Charles was a breath of fresh air.
From the first day of his Restoration
He renewed the spirit of the nation.
We've alluded to the celebration –
Colourful, ecstatic, spontaneous –
That attended his return. Without fuss,
And by example, Charles turned back the clock.

The theatre

Playgoers had suffered a lethal shock
Under Cromwell. Theatres were closed down,
Players and managers drummed out of town.
But happily Charles adored a good play.
The cobwebs of humbug were swept away
As the new King licensed (such was his way)
Two playhouses: the King's (Drury Lane)
And the Duke of York's. Londoners, again,
Could visit the theatre! Female actors
(A first) now trod the boards, one of the factors,

Rhyming History

For sure, in the revived popularity
Of 'the drama', and the immorality
For which certain do-gooders denounced the stage.

Satirical comedies were all the rage,
Witty and bawdy. Some, like *The Man of Mode*
(By George Etherege), alluded, as in code,
To well-known rogues of the day. Its hero,
Dorimant (sex appeal, ten; morals, zero),
Was the young Earl of Rochester in disguise.
The debauchee in question (surprise, surprise)
Was pleased with this figure, quite flattered in fact.
Amoral, a drunkard, and lacking in tact,
A poet (of sorts) and a cynic to boot,
Rochester was wild. Charles didn't give a hoot.
The Earl was made welcome in the royal 'set'.
Did this disconcert the moralists? You bet!

Charles the Second and the Restoration

Etherege, too, was a pal. The King, you see,
Was on terms of easy informality –
Critics claimed a dangerous intimacy –
With artists and poets, playwrights and jockeys
(I kid you not) – even actors, if you please!
Buckingham, his chum since childhood, was a rake
And a rogue. He made a serious mistake
In killing his mistress's husband, the snake.
Did he die for his crime? It was make or break.
No, the villain was pardoned, for goodness' sake.

I'm appalled. Charles excused Monmouth, his own son,
In comparable circumstances. No one –
I repeat, no one, be he pauper or King –
Should condone such infamy. You'll be thinking
That Charles was lucky to get away with it.

His reputation did suffer, bit by bit –
Not that he much cared. He was easy-going
And lax, though there's no real way of knowing
Whether this was the true Charles or a façade.
It's as if, by living well and playing hard,
He kept life's terrors at one remove. The King
Gave little away. Few had any inkling
What lay beneath the surface (if anything) –
What Charles was really up to behind that smile.
My guess is this: that he was fearful all the while
Of the King his father's fate. Those years in exile
Were his education. The subtle art of guile
Was a lesson well learned. He had no wish, he said,
To go travelling again. Charles died in his bed,
Beloved of his subjects. Take it as read
That this was no fluke. This King kept his head!

A footnote to 'the drama'. Aphra Behn
Was our first female playwright. Now and then
A woman bucks the trend, and it was she
Who caught the public mood, refreshingly,

Rhyming History

With her comedy, *The Rover.* The plot
Follows one Willmore, based on John Wilmot,
Earl of Rochester. We met him above,
Our hero from *The Man of Mode*, in love
(Or rather in lust) – thus immortalised,
Twice, on the English stage. You'll be surprised
To learn that Behn was a government spy,
Working undercover in Holland. Why,
One wonders, did they take no cognisance
Of her warning (based on reconnaissance)
Of Dutch plans for their raid on the Medway?
She sent her despatch, but made no headway.
They ignored her. How? A woman, perhaps?
That sort of thing should be left to the chaps.

Literature

From drama to literature. John Milton
Was the great poet of his age; John Bunyan,
The master of prose; each one a Puritan.
So far removed were they from bawdy plays,
The contrast never ceases to amaze.
Yet they share, broadly, the same 'time window':
The divine epic and the smutty show.
The point is a far from trivial one.
That the same era could embrace Milton
And, say, George Etherege, or Wycherley
(The latter a tad later), seems to me
To speak volumes in the royal favour.
Charles preferred works of a coarser flavour,
But never showed himself tyrannical
Concerning matters puritanical.

He was a strong advocate, you'll recall,
Of 'indulgence'. When they wouldn't play ball
(Parliament, I mean), the King just shrugged
And moved on. But he refused to be mugged.

Charles the Second and the Restoration

True to his principles, he'd tolerate
Where possible. To me at any rate,
This is Charles' best legacy. Don't forget
That Milton was a regicide and yet,
Post-Restoration, his life was spared.
Marvell spoke up for him; few others dared.
John was left in peace to write his epic,
His *Paradise Lost*, to be specific –
To "justify the ways of God to men",
And well worth the effort. Ten out of ten!
Milton had some trouble (this isn't rare)
In finding a publisher. Hardly fair.
He hawked it around; they just didn't care.
He finished his poem in '63,
But four years it took (a scandal to me)
To sell the manuscript, ten pounds the fee.
A miserly sum, I'm sure you'll agree.

John Bunyan languished long in Bedford gaol,
An outrage on a more than modest scale.

His policy of preaching publicly
Was his offence. A Nonconformist he,
A Puritan, he posed a threat, you see,

Rhyming History

To the post-Commonwealth Protestant state.
That's how it was perceived, at any rate.
Bunkum, of course, but such was Bunyan's fate.
His masterpiece, that fine allegory,
The Pilgrim's Progress, is Christian's journey
In the form of a dream: his setting out,
His perilous progress, temptation, doubt;
His brushes with Sloth, Mrs. Knownothing,
Money-love, Heedless and Mr. Fearing;
His run-ins with Obstinate, Feeblemind,
Pliable, Brisk and others of their kind;
With lessons learnt from those of fairer face:
Piety, Prudence, Penitence and Grace.
Great-heart, Mr. Self-will and Old Honest
Showed Christian the way. He passed the test!

First published in 1678,
The Progress was a smash hit. The same date
(Give or take a year or two) saw performed
The Man of Mode (or so I've been informed),
The Country Wife (William Wycherley)
And one 'work' (I don't say this bitchily)
By John Wilmot (that's Rochester himself) –
Sodom and Gomorrah. It's on a shelf
In the London Library, believe that
If you will. It's the most dreadful old tat!
I'm surprised it's survived. No Euripides,
Rochester was as different as chalk and cheese
To the other two Johns – little more than a tease.
But did Charles read his Milton? I ask you! Please!

Music, science and philosophy

Church music was restored to its old glory
Under Charles, while science (a success story)
Flourished under the royal patronage.
His reign represented a golden age

Charles the Second and the Restoration

Of new scientific experiment –
A truly exciting development –
In the fields of mechanics, chemistry,
Physics and natural philosophy.
Charles founded the Royal Society
In 1660. The King's interest
In all its workings encouraged the best:
Sir Christopher Wren (a founder member);
John Locke; Robert Boyle (we all remember
Boyle's Law from school); our friend, John Evelyn;
John Dryden, the poet (whose only sin
Was to change religions with the wind);
Robert Hooke, that forgotten *Wunderkind* –
A key figure in the Society,
An expert on optics, geometry,
Architecture, physics, geology,
Town planning, surveying and botany.

Newton fell out with Hooke, whom he accused
Of plagiarism. Hooke was not amused.
To tell the truth, he felt roundly abused.
The theory of gravity, he claimed,
Was his. Yet it's Isaac Newton who's famed
For the breakthrough, the apple and all that.
If Hooke discovered it, I'll eat my hat.

I digress. The Royal Society.
Its brief was broad. Therein lay its glory:
Agriculture, meteorology,
Navigational research, history.
Witness, indeed, the catholicity
Of its members: philosophers, playwrights,
Gardeners, diarists, poets. By rights,
It should have failed the 'specialist' test.
Instead, its very range brought out the best.

This lends a far more enlightened context
To the King's private conduct. Oversexed,

Rhyming History

Yes; but there was no sinister subtext.
Critics will seize on the slightest pretext
To traduce a King's character. In truth,
Charles was a moral chap. I hear you. "Strewth!"
You cry. I'll defend my opinion.
His poor dear wife was no mere minion.
He adored her. When it came to the crunch,
Catherine's enemies ate her for lunch –
The anti-Catholic faction, I mean,
Fanatics all. Yet Charles stood by his Queen,
Refused to divorce her, 'put her away'
(Easily done). To his credit, I say.

Sport and recreation

Charles liked to keep fit. The King led the way
In outdoor pursuits. He swam every day.
Tennis he loved, and excelled at pall-mall
(*Pêle-mêle*, some say), played with racquet and ball –
A boisterous form of croquet, that's all.
Riding became a particular passion.
Racing at Newmarket was well in fashion
By the late 1660s. Twice each year
Charles and his *entourage* set up camp here,
Ministers and mistresses. Work? No fear.
Raise a glass to the Sport of Kings! Hear, hear!

Charles, too, was a prodigious walker.
Sedentary, he was no great talker –
But a quick turn around St. James's Park,
He could talk the hind legs off… What a lark!
With the odd adviser trotting behind,
He managed more business, I think you'll find,
On his brisk, early morning promenade
Than sitting at home in his own backyard.

He designed St. James's Park, by the way,
The best royal landscaper of his day.

Charles the Second and the Restoration

Charles created a lake in the French style –
Ever the quintessential Francophile –
Stocked it with fish (a fertile habitat
For water fowl, wild geese and birds like that,
Moorhens and ducks) and threw open its gates
To his loyal subjects. One hesitates
(Knowing that) even to dare criticise.
Charles was far nobler than folk realise.

P.S. Do visit St. James's Park today
To see the pelicans. In their own small way
They represent a curious legacy
From the days of old. For good King Charles, you see,
Accepted from Russia, as a present,
A pair of breeding pelicans. This event
Was felicitous. It's our link with the past.
History has the power to flabbergast.

Charles and the Catholics

We took a break from the hullabaloo
Of politics in March '72.

Rhyming History

It's time to return to the daily grind.
I'm quietly confident that we shall find
Much of interest to entertain us.

Parliament kicked up a rare old fuss
Over the King's second Declaration
Of Indulgence. Members' indignation
Was intense. Charles proposed, off his own bat –
He was dubbed for his pains an autocrat –
The suspension of England's penal laws
Against Catholics. If they stayed indoors,
They could worship as they pleased: a fine thing,
And a just, to my way of reckoning.

Imaginations ran riot. What if
Charles 'converted'? Almost as bad, what if
The Duke of York already had? What if
The Papists took over? What if… what if… ?
Protestants panicked. Folk were scared stiff.

Statistics suggest (I reckon they're right)
That Catholics were hardly dynamite.
A mere one *per cent* of the populace
(Max.) shared their faith. The laws were a disgrace,
A cruel, intrusive aberration.
Charles commands my total admiration.

The King, however, never stood a chance.
His ill-considered alliance with France –
Though people didn't know the half of it –
Against the Dutch gave the Commons a fit.
What timing! What nerve! What folly, I say!
With Holland striving to hold France at bay
(The Dutch were Protestant), there was no way
That Parliament would vote ready cash
With no strings attached. To call the King rash
Was the great understatement of the age,
No contest. For when Charles first took the stage,

Charles the Second and the Restoration

He exuded confidence. He refused
To compromise his Indulgence. Amused
He was not. Well, nor was Parliament.

Members expressed themselves less than content.
The Commons would countenance no supplies
Until Charles backed down, which (surprise, surprise)
He was forced to, unequivocally.
The Declaration was ditched. Happily,
The King displayed an elasticity
In his make-up that his father, sadly,
Had lacked (and that his brother might gladly
Have learned). So, it seems, even-handedly,
Charles dropped his reforms. Sorry and sickening.

War with the Dutch

Parliament had been prorogued by the King
In '71. It's fairly amazing,
But Charles not only launched his Declaration
In its absence, but committed the nation
To his Dutch campaign. This is hard to forgive.
But war fell within the King's prerogative.
The theory obtains today. As I live,
The Prime Minister (in the Queen's name, of course)
Enjoys the prerogative (without recourse
To Parliament) to launch hostilities
On any country he chooses – I mean, please!
His government would soon be brought to its knees
Without the support of the Commons, okay;
But that's the law as it still stands, come what may.

It was far more straightforward in King Charles' day.
Foreign affairs could be directed his way –
Provided, that is, he was able to pay.
His prorogued Parliament wasn't recalled
Until '73. The King was appalled

145

At the patent lack of support for the war.
The campaign had been launched a full year before.
From the moment, however, the fighting began
It was plain that poor England was an also-ran.

The French, to our shame, made most of the running –
Not just a matter of simple out-gunning,
They were better equipped, far more inventive,
With (sad to say) a much stronger incentive.
Louis the Fourteenth had massive ambition.
His naval force was in cracking condition;
His landed troops, too, posed a terrible threat.

But before the French managed to close the net,
The desperate Hollanders opened their dykes –
The mother, I should say, of preventive strikes –
And flooded their land. They refused to give in,
The Dutch. Good for them. In the long run they'd win.

Charles the Second and the Restoration

The English fleet enjoyed no victories.
All three navies suffered fatalities
Far in excess of expectations: Dutch,
English and French. Our dishonour was such
That in early summer, at Southwold Bay –
It's 1672, by the way –
Our fleet, in a state of sad disarray,
Was sorely punished by the nimble Dutch.

The French, of course, didn't suffer as much.
They were better prepared and better led.
For the Duke of York, it has to be said
(Commander of the Fleet), was forced, I've read,
To abandon ship not just once, but twice –
To save his own skin. One who paid the price,
One who made the ultimate sacrifice,
Was the Earl of Sandwich. A fine tribute
Was paid by Evelyn, his friend: astute,
"Of a sweet obliging temper" and "chaste",
Sandwich was never known to act in haste,
For which "prudence" and "dedication"
He acquired a tarnished reputation.

The Duke of Albemarle was a critic,
As was Lord Clifford (ever the cynic).
No "great opinion" had either man
Of the 1ˢᵗ Earl. Evelyn was a fan,
This is clear. The "heady expedition"
Of Clifford he deplored. The condition
Of our fleet had ever been of concern
To Sandwich. Albemarle would never learn,
So "brutish" and "stupidly furious"
Was the arrogant Duke. Inglorious,
Then, was Sandwich in his enemies' eyes,
"Because he was not rash". It's no surprise
That he was "utterly against the war"
From the beginning. Yet he knew the score.

Rhyming History

He'd pay the price for his opposition.
Indeed, it was Evelyn's suspicion
That he did. Seeing the brave Earl "engaged",
The "stoutest of the rest" (John is enraged)
"Durst not come to his succour, or would not".
Some reckon Sandwich deserved all he got.
Not I, nor Evelyn (he sounds pretty cross),
Who was "heartily grieved at this mighty loss".

He's prepared to go further. His friend died
(This is some charge) to "gratify the pride
"And envy of some I named". Well, that's war,
I'd say, and politics. Both I abhor.

The war drifted on. Nobody seemed keen.
The French were in the ascendant. We've seen
How the Dutch managed to hold them at bay,
Just. Both would live to fight another day.

William of Orange (Charles' young nephew)
Had been appointed, quite out of the blue,
Captain General of the Dutch forces.
It's clear, from an abundance of sources,
That he fast made his mark. Then Johann de Witt –
Who'd frankly never been much of a hit –
Was assassinated. The culprit? Well,
An interesting question… hard to tell.
William had nothing to do with it,
Though never the greatest fan of de Witt.
In short, within months of his promotion
Will became, without further commotion,
New 'Stadtholder' of the States General.

So, as well as Captain and Admiral,
He was nominated, at twenty-one,
Supreme leader of the Dutch. Not much fun,
You might imagine, at that age. His fame,
Nonetheless, spread apace, as his good name,

Respected and feared, became a by-word –
In that age of zealots far from absurd –
For freedom and the Protestant ethic.
His early prospects? Frankly, pathetic –
With Louis of France breathing down his neck…
And war with Uncle Charles… Well, what the heck:
In for a guilder, as the saying goes.
How William made it, God only knows.

But make it he did. When Charles sought an accord –
He'd run out of money; his subjects were bored –
William didn't even deign to reply.
Charles was too haughty, that was one reason why,
But still a bit naughty in a nephew, what?
William clearly gave as good as he got.

This was awkward. The King was in a cleft stick.
He needed more cash and he needed it quick.
He didn't require Parliament's consent
To declare war, but that's as far as it went.
He certainly did have to go cap in hand
For funds, and it's not that hard to understand
Why Lords and Commons, both, struck a hard bargain.
This was a battle that the King couldn't win.
He had to drop, as we've seen, his hobbyhorse –
His precious Declaration. We, of course,
Three hundred and forty-odd years down the line,
Are still the poorer for the stubborn, asinine
Posture of this Cavalier Parliament.
I'd often wondered what 'Cavalier' meant.
Well, now I'm the wiser, I can rest content.

More anti-Catholic sentiment

Not only was the King obliged to drop
His reforms, but the Commons (in a strop)
Introduced (and quickly passed) a Test Act:
Humiliation for Charles, that's a fact.

Rhyming History

He'd no choice but to signify assent.
A vengeful Parliament was hell-bent,
With venom, on rooting out Catholics
From public office. Up to their old tricks,
The Lords and Commons (Anglican, mainly)
Required, by the Act (malice, quite plainly),
All office holders to swear, publicly,
Various oaths pledging allegiance
To the Church of England. Here was a chance
To clobber the Catholics! Forget France,
Forget the war, forget royal finance:
Smoke out the wretched Papists! Make 'em dance!

Credit this: office holders were required –
In public, appropriately attired
And, most importantly (all down to spite),
Strictly according to Anglican rite –
To take Holy Communion: a test
Of their adherence, plain and manifest,
To the Anglican Church. No Catholic,
However able, loyal, heroic
Or true, could continue to serve the King
As a servant of the state. Sickening.

The measure was the perfect opposite
Of Charles' Declaration. It made him spit.
Nothing, he knew, could be done about it.
He signed (no option) on the dotted line.
He sighed. He figured who'd have to resign –
His brother, for one. For James, Duke of York,
Was a convert. There'd already been talk
And now he was ready to 'take a walk',
As they say. Lord High Admiral? No more!
He left office in June. Clifford, for sure,
Was another Papist shown the door.
He resigned his post as Lord Treasurer –
Or was thrown to the wolves, if you prefer.

He may have been ruthless and rather grand,
But Thomas was loyal. He was unmanned
By the shock of his downfall. We understand
That he met his death, sadly, by his own hand.

The tide of anti-Catholicism
Was fierce. It smacks of no heroism
For a Catholic to take his own life –
A mortal sin, I think. The mental strife,
The torment, attendant on such an act
Suggests, however, that poor Clifford lacked
No courage. The Test Act made this impact:
To isolate and to stigmatise. Well,
I trust that brave Lord Clifford was spared hell.

The King meanwhile soldiered blithely on.
It's now '73. Clifford was gone.   **1673**
Shaftesbury (who supported the Test Act)
Was soon, for his pains, to find himself sacked.
The Cabal was breaking up. Charles' old chum
Buckingham, ever a pain in the bum,
Was putting out hostile feelers. The cause?
Catholicism! They deserve applause
For their very nerve. Could the King care less?

It appears not. For his latest mistress,
Louise de Kéroualle (this we have seen),
Was a staunch Catholic. Was Charles so green
That he failed to smell danger? My best guess
Is that he was, though I have to confess
That the mind of this King is hard to read.

Mary of Modena

If he was aware, then he paid scant heed.
Things turned nasty (very tricky indeed)
When James, Duke of York, with indecent speed,

Rhyming History

Married a fifteen-year-old Catholic,
Mary of Modena. I feel quite sick,
For James by now was a crusty old stick –
Lecherous, forty and running to fat.
No one, it seems, cared a fig about that.
They dubbed the poor girl "daughter of the Pope"
And called upon the King himself (some hope)
To disavow the match. Another nail,
They feared, in the Protestant coffin. Hail,
The Catholic succession! James (take heed)
Was heir to the throne. So, should Mary breed
And bear a son, the Protestant nightmare
Would become reality. In despair,
Those most deeply opposed to 'Papistry',
To all things foreign and 'arbitrary' –
Such men embraced our good friend Shaftesbury –
Proposed an alternative strategy.

Let the King remarry, produce an heir,
And eclipse his brother's 'family'. There,
Problem solved! There was just one flaw, of course.
The Queen was living, as strong as a horse!
Easily managed: arrange a divorce –
Shaftesbury's solution. Even more crass
Was Buckingham's input. He (silly ass)
Suggested having Catherine kidnapped,
Then, once she was suitably 'handicapped',
Dumping her for desertion! Madder still,
And further proof of Buckingham's ill will,
Was to ship her to America! What?
It seems that the Duke was losing the plot.

James' marriage went ahead. The poor girl
Had never heard of England. In a whirl –
Her chosen career was that of a nun –
Mary disembarked at Dover. No one,
We're told, but no one, rode over to greet her,
Though James, I imagine, turned out to meet her.

Peace

Parliament became ever more tetchy,
Suspicious and obstinate. It's sketchy,
The picture over the next two or three years,
But one thing is certain: it ended in tears.
Commons and Lords were increasingly intent
On peace with the Dutch. The King expressed content,
But he told a gross lie to Parliament
When he assured members (here he took a chance) –
I quote – "there is no other Treaty with France
"Either before or since, not already printed,
"Which shall not be made known". I've earlier hinted
That Charles the Second chose to draw quite a fine line
Between truth and falsehood, but here he showed no sign

153

Of honesty, integrity or probity.
Fair's fair, he couldn't reveal the Dover Treaty,
Not at this late stage; but such a bare-faced porkie,
Such brazen twisting of the truth, from England's King,
Was positively Nixonian. Quite breathtaking!

Much good did it do him. Parliament,
Demonstrating a rising discontent
With the war, refused to release more cash
And demanded peace. Fearing a backlash
(He loathed confrontation), the King backed down.
He "desired peace with Holland" (what a clown),
Always had done, a lasting peace to boot.
What of Louis? Charles didn't give a hoot,
It appeared, for his old obligations
Under the Dover Treaty. Relations
Became somewhat strained (hardly surprising)
Between Charles and his cousin, the French King.

The English settled for peace with the Dutch –
The Treaty of Westminster. In a wry touch,   **1674**
Cousin Charles pleaded shortage of money
As his motive (pathetic or funny?).
Louis swallowed this lame excuse, if you please,
And in due course offered renewed subsidies.

Thomas Osborne, Earl of Danby

Peace with the Dutch was facilitated
By Sir Thomas Osborne. Underrated
By history (I'm something of a fan),
Osborne's topsy-turvy career began
In 1665 as the MP
For York; then Treasurer of the Navy
In '68; and, by '73,
Lord High Treasurer. The Earl of Danby
He became in early '74.

Charles the Second and the Restoration

Rapid promotion indeed. The Dutch war
Offended Danby's sensibilities.
He subscribed to all the old loyalties:
An unshakeable trust in monarchy,
A strong, Protestant foreign policy –
Danby was fiercely anti-French, you see –
And robust Anglicanism at home.
He'd no time at all for the Church of Rome.
Today we'd call him a High Church Tory.

Party politics (another story),
Albeit in an embryonic state,
Were starting to stir. Whigs, at any rate –
Named after Scottish rebels, 'Whiggamores' –
Were the first; then, after a decent pause,
Came Tories, called after Irish bandits
(Who knew that, then? Hands up!). Whigs were the pits,
Opined Danby, Shaftesbury's successor.
He had a point. Danby is the lesser,
By reputation, of the two. Well, we'll see.
Shaftesbury was a monster, it seems to me.

Of this maverick there'll be more anon.
Inclined to sulk and to feel put upon,
His new (unofficial) position
Was to head the 'country' opposition.
Shaftesbury was deft at criticising.
One chronicler (this isn't surprising)
Focused on his "wonderful faculty
"At opposing" (which he did splendidly)
"And running things down". He had not "the like force
"In building up". This was his ruin, of course.

Danby enjoyed an initial success
In matters financial. I confess,
He had luck on his side. A boom in trade
Boosted revenues; but savings were made,

155

Rhyming History

On Danby's initiative, at Court;
In the Navy, where swingeing cuts were sought;
And by slimming down the Army. In short,
A radical programme of retrenchment
Was launched. Yet Charles was ever dependent
On his long-suffering Parliament.
He'd always, alas, been short of money.
Danby was a far from happy bunny
On the vexed question of Charles' mistresses —
Ever a drain on the royal finances.
Quarrel with Kéroualle? Don't even try,
Was the message loud and clear and that's why,
Perhaps, Danby never really succeeded,
And Commons' supply was regularly needed.

This dependence was painfully evident
In a speech by the King to Parliament
In April '75. The Navy   **1675**
Was in sad disrepair. Members maybe,
Just maybe, might feel inclined to stump up?
They feared, as ever, being sold a pup.
For Charles had troops still fighting on behalf
Of the French King. Was he having a laugh?

Astride a most precarious see-saw,
Charles appeared ready to prepare for war —
In the Dutch interest now, against France —
But simultaneously took his chance
By floating negotiations, again,
With Louis for fresh subsidies. In vain?
Not a bit of it! Cloaked in secrecy,
Charles concluded a new three-year treaty   **1676**
With the French — breathtaking duplicity
On a stupendous scale. Did Danby know?
Probably. How could he not? I'm sure, though,
That he sought to make his royal master
See sense. Yet who suffered the disaster?

Danby, of course. No one said politics
Was fair. This, though, was a most heady mix.

Charles effectively stood on the sidelines
For the next year or so. Louis' designs
On Holland, aggressive and persistent,
Developed apace. Charles was resistant,
As ever, to committing his forces
In support of the Dutch. His resources
Were such as to furnish a fine excuse.
Covertly, of course, it was the French noose,
The stranglehold of his royal cousin,
That shackled Charles. He simply couldn't win.

Come out for William in open war?
Louis would blow the gaff. Charles knew the score.
Should the Treaty of Dover become known
(Its Catholic clause, at least), then his throne,
His character, indeed his very life
Were in jeopardy. A Catholic wife,
A Catholic mistress, both bad enough –
But as nothing to Louis cutting up rough.
For Charles to be caught in bed with the French King,
In the arms of France (figuratively speaking),
Were to spell the end of his glorious reign:
The Civil War played out all over again.

William of Orange

Meanwhile, plodding doggedly on through thick and thin,
There was William. He knew, to save his skin,
That he had to keep old Uncle Charles on side.
To fight alone against France were suicide.
Will, to be frank, was pretty apprehensive.
The threat posed by France was real, extensive
And pressing. The Dutch were on the defensive.
As such, they were in dire need of allies.
A marriage alliance (surprise, surprise)

Might fit the bill. It's easy to criticise,
But he tried on his cousin Mary for size.

She proved a good fit. Firstly, she was Charles' niece;
Secondly, she was a pretty little piece
(This counted); thirdly, most important of all,
She was Protestant. Will had met a brick wall
When, with Danby's enthusiastic support
And the backing of Parliament, he'd sought
To commit Charles to declaring open war
Against France (we know why Charles chose to ignore
The request). But, when it came to a wedding,
The King was all for his young nephew bedding
His brother's daughter. The sooner the better!
Second in line, Will was lucky to get her!

The marriage of Princess Mary   1677

Poor child, she was fifteen if she was a day.
Nobody thought to consult her, anyway:
Sacrificed on the altar of politics.
Mary collapsed in a fit of hysterics
When she caught a first glimpse of her 'intended':
Plain, shy and short! Well, "least said, soonest mended",
As they say. This marriage, against all the odds,
Turned out a success. All in the lap of the gods!

The wedding was a Dutch *coup,* have no doubt.
Louis was furious when he found out:
Charles' niece, hitched to his mortal enemy!
In revenge, he stopped the French subsidy –
In the event, just temporarily.
The King defended himself airily:
The marriage plans had been Heaven-sent;
It was strongly not his professed intent
To wrong-foot his cousin Louis, his friend.

It was largely, however, to this end
That Charles (the rogue) proposed an alliance
With Holland, Austria and Spain – against France!
This appeared utter lunacy, at first glance,
Given the King's vulnerability
Over (you guessed it) the Dover Treaty.
Yet this piece of back door diplomacy
Seemed to work its magic, however rash,
As Louis shut up and stumped up more cash.

Whatever Charles chose to do, however –
And there's no denying he was clever –
Parliament treated him with distrust.
They might respect Danby, who (dry as dust)
Had proved a wizard with the King's money,
But they feared him. Rather less than funny
Was his avowed intent, as they saw it,
To make the King (they couldn't ignore it)
Independent and self-sufficient.
Ironically, the more efficient
Danby became, and the more proficient
At handling Charles' domestic affairs,
The more likely it was that, unawares,
Parliament would be made redundant.
Their fears, in short, were superabundant:
That his Majesty become 'absolute'
(Like Louis) and a Catholic to boot.

The power of France was given a boost   **1678**
By the Peace of Nymegen. Who ruled the roost?
Not William, certainly. Less than sure
Of the terms of the Peace, he had to endure
The occupation by Louis of land
That was Dutch by right. You should understand
That Will had little choice. He was worn out,
Completely exhausted, simply no doubt.

Rhyming History

The Popish Plot

Fear of Catholics was utter rot.
Here in England, though, like it or not,
The stage was set for the Popish Plot.

August that year was very, very hot,
With London as oppressive as it got.
One Titus Oates, a thoroughly bad lot,
And Israel Tonge (a dangerous clot)
Hatched a most frightening conspiracy.
Since there was no plot, in reality,
They set about to invent one. The King
Was to be murdered – whether by stabbing,
Shooting or poisoning was left unclear,
But never mind. The Pope, it would appear,
Was behind it, the odd Catholic peer,
And the Archbishop of Dublin (oh, dear),
With Louis of France bringing up the rear!

It leaves me feeling not a little queer
That Titus Oates was thought to be sincere,
A truthful and dependable witness.
His fabrication was not just witless,
But fantastic. Charles' assassination
Would trigger immediate invasion,
It was claimed, by France. Jesuits, of course,
Were in on the act; the Irish, perforce;
And Catholics by the score. The King's horse,
For all I know, was party to the plot:
They'd have swallowed that too, as like as not.

Amazingly, Tonge and Oates were believed.
It's astonishing how much they achieved
By sinister lies and innuendo.
They simply sowed the seeds and watched them grow.
Papists were unpopular. Even so,

Charles the Second and the Restoration

It still appears quite staggering to me
That the 'plot' developed quite so lethally.

Yet, throughout the seventeenth century,
The modest, Catholic minority
Was ever subject to persecution,
Discrimination and retribution.
Indeed, since Henry the Eighth's dreadful reign,
Relations had been under constant strain.
Men feared Queen Mary all over again –
'Bloody' Mary. They recalled the martyrs,
Burnt at the stake. They had good cause to curse.
They remembered St. Bartholomew's Day,
In France, where Huguenots were led away
And massacred – put to the sword or shot:
Memories rekindled to stir the pot
And fuel the flames of the Popish Plot.

Rhyming History

Rome was the Antichrist. Couldn't folk see?
The age-old Catholic conspiracy
Was alive and well, in the here and now.
The Papists were on the warpath, and how!
The Great Fire of 1666 –
Who started it? Catholic fanatics!
The Duke of York, no shadow of a doubt,
Lit the first fuse. (He helped to put it out,
You'll recall). Even the prosecution
Of Charles the First, and his execution,
Formed part of the Catholic 'solution'.

The anti-Catholic tradition
Ran deep. The Protestant position
Was, by contrast, robust and strong, and yet
Men feared for their lives. The Catholic threat
Was real, pressing and immediate –
In their eyes. One description of the time
Demonstrates this lunacy in its prime.

I'm hard pressed to transpose it into rhyme,
But here goes: "your children torn… limb from limb"
Or "tossed upon pikes" (I said it was grim)
And "your wives prostituted to the lust
"Of every savage bog-trotter". Just?
You must be joking! Naked prejudice…
"Your daughters ravished" (now listen to this)
"By goatish monks… Your own bowels ripped up"
(Could this be written in true earnest? Yup!)
With "your dearest friends flaming in Smithfield".
Papists' revenge! The Protestants' fate sealed!
Lastly, "holy candles made of your grease":
I like to see that as the centrepiece.
Forget "the joyful sounds of Liberty",
For "this, gentlemen, is Popery".

The fact that folk took this seriously
Goes some way to explain, it seems to me,

Charles the Second and the Restoration

The ease with which the alleged plot took root.
Parliament soon joined in hot pursuit
Of the hare released by Oates and his ilk.
Hatred of Papists was as mother's milk
To the average Protestant die-hard.
Nor were such zealots like to disregard
The heir to the throne's recent conversion
To the Church of Rome. Their plain aversion
To Louise, the King's Catholic mistress,
Had been trumped by the Duke of York's *finesse*
In marrying young Mary Beatrice.
Added to this, Charles caused further distress
By his blatantly pro-French policies,
Openly contemptuous, if you please,
Of his long-suffering Parliament.

Small wonder members nodded their assent
At this "hellish plot" (whatever that meant)
For "subverting" (their word) the government,
"Carried on… for the assassinating…
"By the popish recusants" of the King.

It struck such a raw nerve, that was the thing.
Even Andrew Marvell, level-headed
And astute (the great poet), was wedded
To the crazy notion of a "design"
By the Catholics, corrupt and malign,
To overthrow the lawful government
Of England. The Papists would be content
Only with the "absolute tyranny"
(Andrew's own phrase) of "downright Popery".

So where was the hard evidence? Nowhere.
There was none. And nobody seemed to care.
Fear played its part. Believe this if you will:
Parliament decreed (a bitter pill)
That anyone with the temerity
To question the plot's authenticity

Rhyming History

Did so in danger of his life. Justice?
I don't think so. Pure, naked prejudice.

There was an investigation, of sorts,
Into Oates' allegations. Those spoilsports,
Reason and Truth, seem to have been dismissed,
As the Privy Council couldn't resist
The fine detail of Oates' testimony.
Charles was there in person, and it was he
Who drew attention to obvious flaws
In the evidence. Titus drew applause,
Though, the wilder his accusations grew.
What knavery there was to know, Oates knew!

The trial of Edward Coleman

Two strokes of luck poured fuel on the flames.
Edward Coleman was just one of the names
Fired off with the ease of a scattergun
By Oates and his cronies. The damage done
In tragic Edward's case was far from fun.
Coleman was personal secretary
To the Duchess of York. I have to say
(It sticks in my throat), he was indiscreet,
A time-serving traitor, villain and cheat.
For years, at least, he'd been sending letters
To Jesuits abroad, his abettors
In Catholic plans to further the cause
In England. Of course, this broke all the laws.
His treacherous correspondence was seized.

Titus, we know, was enormously pleased.
The timing was perfect. At Coleman's trial,
No one, but no one, believed his denial
Of a role in the 'plot'. Guilty he was,
For sure, but because (and only because)
Of those treasonous letters. He'd no link,
At all, with the plot. But what do you think?

His guilt was most manifest proof, you bet,
That 'moves' were afoot. When in court they met
(Oates and Coleman, that is) Titus, we're told,
Failed to know it was him. The blood runs cold.

The murder of Sir Edmund Berry Godfrey

The second fortuitous circumstance
Was the dreadful murder (a foul mischance)
Of the very magistrate who had heard
Oates' first deposition. Every word,
Every trumped-up, crazed allegation,
Every lunatic fabrication,
Had been laid before the Justice of the Peace,
Sir Edmund Berry Godfrey. A masterpiece
Of timing! Godfrey's murdered body was found,
Face down, stabbed through the back, on secluded ground
On Primrose Hill – in a ditch, to be exact.
His death was unexplained. Had he been attacked
By footpads? Hardly: his jewels were intact,
As was his money. His pocket book had gone,
But what of that? As murky as Acheron
Was the mystery and remains so today,
A secret of history. Oh, by the way,
Sir Edmund had been run through with his own sword,
Though two surgeons attested, for the record,
That the deceased had most likely been strangled
Before his corpse was subsequently mangled.

Suicide was thought a possibility –
Poor Godfrey had been a depressive, you see.
He must, though, have been remarkably clever
To throttle himself, then stab… Well, whatever…
Sir Edmund Berry Godfrey's death has never,
To this day, been explained. The mob, however,
Surged to the conclusion that suited it best:
The assassins were Catholic. No contest.

Rhyming History

Even John Evelyn, it must be confessed,
Wrote that he'd been strangled, "as was manifest,
"By the Papists". And this the same Evelyn
Who reckoned Titus Oates a "bold" specimen,
"And in my thoughts furiously indiscreet".
Oates may well have been a liar and a cheat,
Yet he caused the public mood to overheat.
The "Roman Catholics were exceeding bold" –
So, not just Titus. The whole nation, we're told,
Was altogether in a "fermentation"
Against them. The imminent expectation
Was of a Catholic rising, invasion
By France, or a terrific conflagration –
A second Great Fire. Lunacy, of course.
The fear that Papists could take England by force
Was pure, unadulterated madness.

Titus Oates

Few men could match Titus Oates for badness.
An utter scoundrel, the greatest sadness
Is that folk believed him so readily.

His pride, wealth and renown grew steadily
As his fevered accusations took hold
On an ever eager populace. Bold
He was indeed, as Evelyn attests.
His testimony led to the arrests,
Among others, of five Catholic peers –
All innocent. Nobody, it appears,
Sought to investigate the evidence
(So-called) against them. It made perfect sense
To send them to the Tower. There they stayed
(Those who lived) for five years. Charles was dismayed,
But kept his head down. What else could he do?
He faced a *tsunami* and this he knew.

Charles the Second and the Restoration

Titus was fêted wherever he went.
The more mischief he contrived to invent,
The higher he rose. With his own armed guard,
The rogue evinced a lofty disregard
For facts. He never told the truth at all!
He was given apartments in Whitehall,
Rent free, and granted a special pension,
With extra perks too many to mention.

Oates boasted a most unprepossessing
Figure. Short and squat (sorry, no messing),
His five double chins wobbled as he walked
And his high-pitched voice sounded, when he talked,
Like some strange bird. He didn't speak, he squawked.
The least appealing feature (a disgrace)
Was his mean mouth, set halfway up his face.
His vast forehead, his tiny piggy eyes
And pudgy, button-mushroom nose gave rise

Rhyming History

To the image of a freak. Now, I've read
These descriptions which, it has to be said,
Are shameful, base and of little credit
To the historians. There, I've said it.
As if a chap's less than handsome image
Should suggest… At the risk of a scrimmage,
These poisonous portraits, sadly, to me,
Are sleazy, outdated (and non-PC).

Be that as it may. I'm no fan at all
Of Oates, the man. The nation was in thrall
To rumour and fantasy, plots and schemes,
Catholic intrigue and dangerous dreams.
Books were burnt, the houses of Papists sacked,
And innocent reputations attacked.
Here was a picture of a world gone mad.
Even Samuel Pepys (this is quite sad)
Was sent to the Tower – the cause, I fear,
His 'closeness' to James, Duke of York. Oh, dear.
The end of a blameless naval career?
Pepys suffered guilt by association
With his boss. I have no hesitation
In saying that England had taken leave
Of her senses. Well, that's what I believe.

Edward Coleman, with far better reason,
Was arraigned, convicted of High Treason
And executed. The killing season,
Moreover, continued with the trial
Of Godfrey's three 'butchers'. The denial
Of guilt by this unfortunate trio
Was rejected with relish (nay, brio)
By the jury, those 'twelve good men and true'.
Scapegoats were needed. What else could they do?

Thirty-five victims, at the very least,
Were 'sacrificed' (including the odd priest)

In the months when the deadly Popish Plot
Was at its awful height. Like it or not,
The King kept a low profile. He was wise.
He contemplated "with tears in my eyes"
The patent injustice perpetrated
On his blameless subjects. He created
No extra waves. Rather, he applied balm
To his kingdom's wounds and remained quite calm.

Further exclusion of Catholics

Here's just one example of what I mean.
Parliament moved (I find this obscene)
That no Catholic be eligible
To sit as a member. Negligible
This was not, for the measure, it appears,
Was designed to bar all Catholic peers,
Including James, Duke of York, the King's heir.
Charles, and James himself, thought "Whoa! Stop there!" –
The thinnest end of the wedge. Danby sought,
On the King's behalf (and with his support),
To urge the fiery Parliament
To make an exception of James. Charles went,
In person, to the Lords to give his word –
Or "to assure you" (the phrase he preferred) –
That he was prepared to give his assent
To all "reasonable bills" (what this meant,
I'm unsure), but only to this extent:
"So as they tend not to impeach the right
"Of succession" (this was dynamite,
Touching James) nor of "any Protestant
"Successor". The King's speech was resonant
Of balance, fairness and perfect good sense.

The last to believe all this 'plot' nonsense,
Charles was nonetheless forced (in part) to bow
To members' whims, but would never kowtow.

Rhyming History

So, anti-Catholic proclamations
Were issued in force. The protestations
Of recusants were ignored by the King,
As anti-Papist laws, if anything,
Were enforced with unusual rigour.
Was this a sign of weakness or vigour
On Charles' part? Most decidedly, I'd say,
The latter. He and Danby won the day.
By a tiny majority (just two)
James was exempt from the excluded (phew!) –
The one who got away! Charles had the knack
Of knowing exactly when to sit back:
Defence, the subtlest form of attack.

The Queen accused

'Exclusion', as such, was some months away.
Vultures were circling. As was his way,
The King in his wisdom kept them at bay.
All this we shall see. The point to make now
Is that events were conspiring (and how!)
To undermine Charles at every turn.
His seeming air of relaxed unconcern
Deceived his critics. He dug in his toes
When the Queen was accused. No one quite knows
How Oates was so stupid, utterly crass,
"Presumptuous" (Evelyn's word), the ass,
As to 'credit' Catherine with a plot
To poison her husband. Treasonous rot!

The King, with a clear view of what was what,
Dismissed this rubbish. He had Oates, the clot,
Locked in his rooms. A recalcitrant lot,
The Council released him. How about that?
It just goes to show how the King's *diktat*
In times of stress ran a limited course,
With his regal power a fragile force.

Charles the Second and the Restoration

Danby targeted

Charles might move mountains to defend his Queen.
He drew the line at Danby. As we've seen,
The Lord Treasurer was quite an asset,
Loyal, an ace economist… and yet
Armies of enemies he made with ease.

Members he bribed (today we call it sleaze)
To support the King's 'Court' party, so-called –
Though to modest effect. Whigs were appalled
At his adherence (uncompromising)
To the concept of an 'absolute' King,
As they saw it. Danby, a loyalist
Through and through, was the classic Royalist:
Anglican, an out-and-out monarchist,
Anti-French and pro-Dutch. You get the gist.

Foreign affairs were Danby's undoing.
For when Charles the Second went a-wooing
(And I'm not talking mistresses this time,
But his French cousin), Danby's alleged crime
Was his acquaintance with this policy –
Nay, the critics claimed, his complicity –
Whilst simultaneously canvasing cash
From Parliament (this decidedly rash)
For war with France in support of the Dutch!

None of this would have mattered very much
Had Danby not been exposed. But found out
He was: dead meat, no shadow of a doubt.
He'd contrived to upset Ralph Montagu –
Ex-Ambassador to Paris to you –
By causing Ralph to be sacked from his post
On the Privy Council. Danby was toast.
Montagu had in his possession
Papers witnessing a succession

Rhyming History

Of negotiations for subsidy
From the French. Danby, ironically,
Was pro-Dutch. But as Charles' servant, sadly,
He was compromised. So, in secrecy,
He pursued the King's pro-French policy.

This proved his Achilles' heel. Shaftesbury,
The snake, with relish led the hue and cry
Against Danby in Parliament. Why?
No love was lost between them, but the King
Was the true target. This was frightening.
Montagu (an MP) came to the House
And read aloud the letters (little louse)
Which manifested Danby's involvement
In dealings with the French. Parliament
Was shocked, excited, scandalised, outraged.
Shaftesbury (ha!) professed himself amazed.

The whole thing smacked of rank hypocrisy.
Montagu was in the pay of Louis
(Yes, the King of France), who hated Danby,
Friend of the Dutch, who'd arranged, famously,
William and Mary's marriage. What sauce!
Danby had shown not the slightest remorse
For his role in this nightmare alliance.
So Louis, spitting death and defiance,
Laboured night and day to bring Danby down.

Loyalties by this time were upside-down:
Shaftesbury in bed with France! The showdown,
When it came, was ugly and clear cut.
The case, quite simply, was open and shut.
Members clamoured for Danby's impeachment.
They balked at double-dealing and concealment.
What did Charles do? He knew that no agreement
Could be reached. So he dissolved Parliament.

This unheralded dissolution meant **1679**
A welcome end (in the Whigs' eyes, Heaven-sent)
To Charles' stubborn Cavalier Parliament.
Of eighteen years' duration, corrupt and tired,
Its effective lease on life had long expired.

Shaftesbury and his cohorts, for quite a time,
Had pressed for elections. Now in his prime,
The hopeful Earl, all subterfuge and slime,
Had, in the age-old fashion of turncoats,
Exploited the motions of Titus Oates.
He'd not devised the plot, you understand,
But he ran with the pack (so underhand)
And could whip up a mob. From where I stand,
Shaftesbury was a born second-rater.
Brainy, it's true, and a fine debater,
The 1st Earl was a Catholic-baiter,
A bigot, a twister and a traitor.
History affords him a better press –
A progressive genius. I confess,
I fail to see it. Nor could I care less.

'Exclusion'

The general election, if you please,
Returned more "worthy" and "honest" MPs –
The descriptions, of course, are Shaftesbury's –
Than those of the 'Court' party. Two to one
Was the rough ratio. The damage done
To the King's cause, you may well imagine,
Was grave. There was not one vote he could win.

The first 'Exclusion' Parliament,
So-called, appeared indeed to be hell-bent
On barring James from the succession.
Shaftesbury offered no concession.

Mere curbs on a Catholic King's powers
Wouldn't do at all. Hours and hours
Of debate led to one clear conclusion:
Lords and Commons voted for Exclusion.
Charles was aghast: chaos and confusion!

Danby to the Tower

James' personal unpopularity,
As a Catholic, out in the country,
Was one thing; legislation to remove
His rights another. Charles didn't approve
Of James – his stubbornness, stupidity
And lack of sense. The Earl of Shaftesbury,
However, was something else. Slippery,
Devious and smug, he pursued Danby
Through the new Parliament. Like a dog
After a rabbit, he went the whole hog:

Charles the Second and the Restoration

Impeachment… Attainder… Come the hour,
The King, to the utmost of his power,
Sought to pardon Danby. To the Tower,
Though, he duly went – for the next five years:
Yet another of those noble careers
In politics which sadly end in tears.
Charles was badly weakened by Danby's fall.
Shaftesbury's tactics pleased him not at all.

Alternatives to James, Duke of York

The first Exclusion Bill targeted James,
And him alone. There were no other names.
The likelihood of other papist claims
Was remote, but the mere fact that the Bill
Was specific (though sending quite a chill
Through both the brothers) seemed to signify
Unease within the ranks of the Whigs. Why?
Well, no one could agree (though they did try)
On who the King's successor ought to be.

The Duke of York's elder daughter, Mary?
Second-in-line and the obvious choice,
The people, some felt, would hardly rejoice
At the prospect of a foreign consort,
Young William of Orange. It was thought –
Quite erroneously, as it turned out –
That, as a crypto-Stuart, he might flout
The will of the people; and furthermore
(Prescient, this) that he would press for war
Against Louis in support of the Dutch.
James' second daughter didn't count for much.
Poor Anne was only thirteen and, as such,
Hardly a creditable candidate.
The two Princesses were, at any rate,
Protestant. There was even talk, by some,
Of Mary as James' guardian. Ho, hum –

Rhyming History

No prizes for guessing how that went down!
There was a third 'contender' for the Crown:
James, Duke of Monmouth, the King's bastard son.
Charles' eldest and favourite, anyone
With any sense saw the insanity
Of his claim. Handicapped by vanity,
Pride and a lack of imagination,
His mere presence could cause a sensation.

'The Protestant Duke', as his fans dubbed him,
Could whip up the fevered mob on a whim.
Famously popular, frightfully dim,
Handsome, athletic (but out on a limb),
Monmouth believed (or, I wonder, did he?)
In his own royal legitimacy.
His father had been married to Lucy,
Simple as that. Charles, of course, denied it.
That, though, wasn't enough to decide it.

The tale of a mysterious 'Black Box',
Containing their marriage lines, would fox
And bedevil opinion for years,
Leading in due course to bloodshed and tears.

A divided, confused opposition
Conspired to bolster the King's position.
He himself picked his way through this minefield
With aplomb. Determined never to yield
To Exclusion, King Charles nonetheless
Behaved in ways which, I have to confess,
Were characterised by a subtleness
Which split his adversaries further still.
Appointing Shaftesbury to his Council,
He sought to neutralise his enemies.
The Marquess of Halifax, if you please
('The Trimmer', they called him), even changed sides.
Having given Charles some pretty rough rides,

He became an overnight advocate
Of limits on 'King' James' powers, dead set
Against outright Exclusion, and yet
No pushover. Useful to Charles? You bet!

The King also worked hard on his brother.
They'd no real respect for each other,
But kept up appearances. Charles first urged
James to give up his faith. This would have purged,
At a stroke, the whole process, root and branch.
The Duke refused. This gave the King *carte blanche*
To send him abroad – to Brussels, in fact.
Charles, at his best, was a master of tact,
A characteristic James sadly lacked.

Charles was ready, at least, to countenance
(Like Halifax) limits on James. This stance
Cut no ice with the ghastly Shaftesbury
And his ilk. The King's nifty strategy
Of bringing the devious Earl on side…
Successful? Well, I'll leave you to decide.

When it came to the vote, Parliament,
At first and second readings, seemed hell-bent
On enacting the Exclusion Bill.
At which point the King, with an iron will,
Prorogued Parliament, then dissolved it!

James, Duke of Monmouth, on the ascendant

Nonetheless, Charles' enemies, bit by bit,
Appeared to be gaining the upper hand.
Monmouth scored a great triumph in Scotland,
Thus weakening (indirectly) James' case.
The Scottish Covenanters, a disgrace,
Had rebelled against the Establishment:
A threat to episcopal government.

Rhyming History

The English Civil War, you may recall,
Was triggered in Scotland. Now a new squall
Quickly developed into a typhoon
With Archbishop Sharp's murder. All too soon,
A Covenanters' revolution
Was in prospect. And the solution?
The King's son James, despatched to sort it out –
A risky business, without a doubt.
For in my humble view the Duke lacked clout.

Be so good as never to accuse me
Of intransigence or obduracy.
For here I'll admit, in all honesty,
With hand on heart and with due modesty,
That Monmouth scored a resounding success.
The Scottish rebels, I have to confess,
Were trounced. Good riddance! It's anyone's guess
What might have followed had the young Duke lost:
Scotland at war, at most terrible cost.

Be that as it may, after Bothwell Brig,
The scene of his exploits, Monmouth talked big.
Yet he demonstrated great clemency
Towards the vanquished (not so dim, you see).
This show of mercy did him no harm at all.
With his fans and followers James walked tall.

Charles was unfazed. Give a man enough rope…
The trouble was, the errant Duke (the dope)
Believed, alas, his own publicity.
Unlike the artful Earl of Shaftesbury,
James was untainted by duplicity.
The arrogant pup wore his heart on his sleeve:
He was destined for greatness, can you believe!

Sir George Wakeman, the Queen's physician,
Found himself in the sad condition

178

Of being accused (by Titus, of course)
Of plotting to poison the King – what sauce!
In his own defence he talked himself hoarse
And, happy to report, his case was won.
Wakeman was innocent. Justice was done.

Now maybe, just maybe, the tables turned
With the case of Sir George, as juries learned
To "follow their consciences" (Scroggs' own phrase,
The Judge at the trial). England's malaise
Was far from cured. Oates had work still to do,
But times were a-changing. A good job too.

The King's illness

With his enemies in some disarray,
The King fell suddenly ill. Lackaday!
His death seemed imminent. James was away,
You'll recall, on the continent. I'd say
That Monmouth, the monster, rejoiced that day.

If so, his joy was somewhat premature.
Charles' expected exit threw some, for sure,
Into turmoil and panic. Civil War
Was yet on the cards, though an outside chance.
Those anti-Catholics who looked askance
At James, Duke of York, as heir to the throne
Were less than certain (as far as is known)
Of a more attractive alternative.
Should the King expire, then something would give,
But no one was quite sure what – as I live,
A dark and dangerous state of affairs.
The Duke of Monmouth might give himself airs,
But James, Duke of York, when it came to heirs,
Was the first in line, and I'll eat my hat
If any sane man would have challenged that.

Rhyming History

Exclusion Bills, Black Boxes – nothing,
When it came to the crunch, I say nothing,
Compared to a true, legitimate King.

They dithered, then called for James. There's a thing!
He hastened back from Brussels, travelling
I believe, overnight. "The King is dead –
"Long Live the King!" You can take it as read
That his Maj recovered. Propped up in bed,
Fed up with soup, he ate game pie instead.

If ever the crisis went to his head,
James never showed it. While Monmouth saw red,
York kept his cool. This was a watershed,
For sure, in the Exclusion caper.
Just as Titus Oates lit the touch paper
To the Popish Plot, so the King's illness
Put paid to some of the rank bitterness

Unleashed by the Exclusion affair.
Meddle with the succession? Have a care
What you wish for! The King was well aware
That he wasn't out of the woods quite yet;
But the outlook was now far brighter, you bet.

James, Duke of York, back in favour

James' position as Charles' successor
Gained strength overnight. The King's blood pressure
Doubtless fell accordingly. The young Duke
(Monmouth, that is) earned a telling rebuke,
Relieved as he was of his appointment
In Scotland. His abject disappointment
Increased when he too was despatched abroad
To the Netherlands. Cynical and bored,
He fell into an unlikely friendship
With William of Orange. Showmanship
Was James' *forte*; warfare and statesmanship
Were William's. Apart from their kinship,
One wonders what they had to talk about.
Both, though, were out to goad Charles, have no doubt.
As for James senior, his recompense
For loyalty, and for his rare good sense
When the King was sick, was to take the place
Of Monmouth in Scotland. Young James lost face,
As his uncle's standing improved apace.

The death throes of Exclusion

Shaftesbury, somewhat unwisely, attacked
York's appointment. For his pains he was sacked
From the Council. What the Earl sadly lacked
Was a sense of perspective. So, of course –
Showing the world how to flog a dead horse –
He stepped up his argument (in the Lords)
For Exclusion. Halifax crossed swords

With his erstwhile ally. Shaftesbury, still,
Staked his life, his all, on the wretched Bill –
Reintroduced into Parliament,
Freshly elected. As far as it went,
The new Bill mirrored its predecessor,
Barring James as the lawful successor
To his brother. The Commons, as before,
Stood in favour. In the Lords it was war!
Halifax and Shaftesbury, head to head,
Battled it out. Again, take it as read
That Shaftesbury would have fought till he bled,
But he suffered defeat – the vote, it's said,
Two to one against. He took to his bed,
Moody and depressed. Exclusion was dead.

The defeat of the Exclusion Bill –
A relief for the King; a bitter pill
For Shaftesbury – was a crucial stage
In Charles' recovery. This cruel age,
Though, had more of its horrors still in store.
Evelyn (our chum) was shocked to the core
By William Howard Stafford's trial –
1st Viscount Stafford. There's no denial
That here was a most monstrous travesty
Of justice (though the last dregs, hopefully,
Of the hellish Popish Plot). Elderly,
Upright and honest, this Catholic peer
Was one of five noble lords named, I fear,
By that proud, perjured, vaunting Chanticleer,
Titus Oates (the villain), as conspiring
(Without rhyme or reason) to kill the King.

Stafford on trial   1680

His trial was an outrageous thing.
The event was staged in Westminster Hall
Before the King, Lords and Commons and all.

Charles the Second and the Restoration

A mere matter of forty years before,
The Hall had doubled as a court of law
In the case of "the great and wise Strafford",
1st Earl – his name differing from Stafford
By a stray 'r'. (Evelyn points this out,
Though you'd already spotted it no doubt).
In both instances the charge was treason –
In Strafford's case, with very good reason.
Ruthless and cunning, it's easy to see
How he came to grief (all in Volume Three).

But Stafford, the victim of perjury,
Prejudice, hatred, naked villainy
And even, I've read, astonishingly,
The envious spite of his family,
Was innocent – a good man through and through.

His trial was pure theatre (nothing new):
The floor of the Hall "with a stage of boards"
Had been elevated to a height. Lords
Sat on "long forms", the Judges on "woolsacks" –
This Evelyn tells us. One of his knacks
Is to set a fine scene. Placed on its own,
At the far end, was "his Majesty's throne".
On the left was a box for "great ladies"
And, above, a gallery, if you please,
"For ambassadors". There was scaffolding
"To the very roof". This was for seating
The House of Commons, who were out in force,
Hoping for a swift conviction, of course.

A splendid spectacle, then. Poignantly,
A box was built so his daughters could see:
Stafford had two. More significantly,
Given the outcome of this grisly case,
There was a special, privileged place
For the "axe-bearer". A perfect disgrace.

Rhyming History

The principal witness was Oates, of course,
Still in favour. With his face like a horse –
Sorry, I've given up feeling remorse
At caricature – he lied through his teeth,
Untruth upon invention. Good grief,
How could conviction hang upon his word,
False and uncorroborated? Absurd.

Stafford was plotting to raise an army
(Allegedly: all completely barmy),
Commissioned, can you believe, by the Pope!
Was one shred of evidence offered? Nope:
Oates' word, plain and simple. "An hypocrite,"
Evelyn calls him. He'd gained some credit
In naming Coleman; but he was "so slight…
"Passionate, ill bred… " (John had it right)
And "impudent" that his "testimony"
Should not be taken, John says, "verily…

"Against the life of a dog". I agree –
Though tough on the canine, it seems to me.

Stafford nonetheless was adjudged guilty,
Thirty-one against, with fifty-five for –
These his fellow peers 'upholding' the law.
Now here's a detail I deeply abhor:
"The axe was turned edgeways towards him". Oh, lor.
I'm near to weeping. What's more eye-watering
Was the sentence: "hanging, drawing, quartering,
"According to form". The King, I'm glad to report,
Tempered this wickedness. Stafford's life was cut short
By beheading. The Viscount died with dignity,
Confident in the blessedness of God's mercy.

The Oxford Parliament   1681

I'm not the only Englishman to shed a tear.
The King was scandalised. Early in the New Year
He dissolved his fickle, short-lived Parliament,
With fresh elections in the spring. A punishment?
Hardly. The Lords (unelected) passed the judgement.
Moreover, Charles had little time for sentiment.

He planned to take a firmer rein on government.
Critics and friends alike wondered at his intent
When he chose Oxford (some sort of experiment?)
For the first sitting of his newly elected
Parliament. The surly Whigs, as expected,
Put on an impressive show of strength. Riding high
(In their eyes), they omitted to ask themselves why
The King was so unusually resistant
To London. Had he lost his nerve? So confident
Were they that they brought their own troops. Imagine that!
Well, so did Charles. If the Whigs expected a spat,
They were nonetheless disappointed. For the King
Had it all worked out. He'd thought of everything.

Rhyming History

Cousin Louis, again, had come to the rescue.
Covert embassies, secret missions, what-have-you,
Had led to new subsidies. For Louis, you see,
Viewed Exclusion with horror. Either Mary –
Or her husband, William, who'd be even worse –
Might follow should James be barred. He wasn't averse,
Entirely, to Monmouth succeeding. Civil War,
The likely consequence, at worst would be a bore,
At best a diversion – enabling France,
Without English interference, to take her chance
Against the Dutch. Monmouth was a Protestant, though,
As were Mary and William. Who was to know,
For certain, how events might possibly turn out
For France should a Protestant succeed? Have no doubt,
Exclusionists were not to Louis' liking.
Were James to win through, there'd be a Catholic King:
Perfect. So he kept the subsidies rolling in.

Louis saw that no English King could ever win
In the teeth of a stubborn Parliament. He,
Louis, had never comprehended, quite frankly,
What exactly this strange 'Assembly' was for.
In France he'd have readily shown it the door,
Yet he had no such worries. His cousin, therefore,
Should be rescued from the vice of Parliament.
So he subsidised Charles anew. This (Heaven-sent)
Proved crucial. The Oxford Parliament met
With the Whigs in the highest of spirits, you bet.
Shaftesbury was almost childishly optimistic
Of success. This was foolishly unrealistic,
Given the conspicuous lack of agreement
With respect to a successor. In the event,
The issue was academic. Charles called their bluff.
Confident in the French embrace, he'd had enough.

In a superb *coup de théâtre*, a showdown,
The King arranged for his robes of state, and his crown,

To be brought in high secrecy to Christ Church Hall,
Where the Lords were met. Little suspecting at all,
The Commons were summoned to the royal presence.
Shaftesbury and his cronies thought Charles had seen sense.
Despite his protestations that he'd never yield
To their demands, his brother's fate, they felt, was sealed.
Monmouth (Shaftesbury's pet) would be legitimised –
That was the surest bet. They were greatly surprised,
Upon entering the Hall, to witness the King
In full regalia, crown and everything –
A sight as awesome as it was astonishing.

King Charles the Second briefly spoke. He was resolved.
Enough was enough. Parliament stood dissolved.

The Whigs had been outwitted. Shaftesbury
Withdrew to lick his wounds. It seems to me
His day was done. Charles appeared to agree.
The Earl had badly overstepped the mark,
Bringing troops to Oxford – not just some lark,
But proof that his bite was worse than his bark.
Dragged from his bed, he was charged with treason
And, I should say, with pretty good reason.
In the event, though, his trial fell flat.
The wretch was acquitted. How about that?
It was stiff with Whigs, the London jury.
The King was incandescent with fury,
But what could he do? A lucky blighter
Was Shaftesbury, but a plucky fighter.

The death of Shaftesbury

Nonetheless, the world was soon the lighter
By one Earl. For in 1682,   **1682**
The following year, he fled (wouldn't you?)
To Holland. He was never a strong man –
And I, as you know, was never a fan –

But when he died, in early '83,
He was merely a curiosity,
A political maverick. For me,
That's all that can be said of Shaftesbury.

The Oxford Parliament was Charles' last.
The Whigs were on the run, and running fast.
Charles was (strictly speaking) obliged by law –
The Triennial Act of '64 –
To summon a Parliament at least
Once every three years. As fears increased
Of the spectre of an 'absolute' King,
The Act soothed such anxieties. Nothing,
However, could be done to enforce it!
Charles, it seems, had been glad to endorse it
When the legislation was first mooted.
With time, though, the Act was less well suited
To his needs. Parliament was a pain,
A thorn in his side, again and again.
After Oxford he'd had his bellyful.

So he chose to ignore the Act. Wilful?
Most certainly, but that's what the King did,
And no one appeared to bat an eyelid.
Nigh on four years passed before his demise,
And no Parliament! Surprise, surprise!
Charles had neutralised his critics fair and square,
And few folk complained, as far as I'm aware.

A stronger King

Following Oxford the King, as I live,
Bold and strong, seized the initiative.
After Parliament's dissolution
Charles was charged with vigour, resolution
And (dare I say it) a kind of cunning.
From now on the King made all the running.

As a first step he ordered to be read
In every church in the land, it's said,
A most patriotic declaration.
This recalled the sore loss to the nation
Of religion (of course), liberty
And (not to be forgotten) property
Suffered in the course of the Civil War,
During which disaster the Church, the Law,
The very Monarchy itself (don't scoff)
Were (to quote the King's own words) "shaken off".
The implication was self-evident:
The Whigs, now in eclipse, had been hell-bent
On fomenting rebellion, schism
And (that nightmare) republicanism.

All nonsense, of course. Even Shaftesbury
Had no wish to destroy the monarchy.
He dreaded "a mechanic tyranny" –
According to Evelyn's *Diary.*

The declaration helped sound the death knell
For Whig dreams. Tories savoured the rare smell
Of success. Other factors helped the King:
In the early 80s trade was booming,
Bringing a boost in royal revenues.
All this conspired to give the Whigs the blues.

The Rye House Plot   1683

Early in the spring of 1683
An alleged plot (Protestant, surprisingly)
Was hatched (the 'Rye House', so-called) against the lives
Of James and the King. One record that survives
Is that of our friend John Evelyn again –
A reliable diarist, in the main,
Though here quick to judge. I'll seek to explain.

Rhyming History

Algernon Sidney was one of the plotters,
And William, Lord Russell – Whigs, the rotters.
The 1st Earl of Essex was in on it too,
And Monmouth to boot (almost certainly true) –
According to Evelyn's musings, at least.
Now Truth's a notoriously fickle beast.
It's highly plausible that this murky plot
Was used as the perfect excuse, like as not,
For a purge of the Whigs. So what exactly
Was the character of this conspiracy?
Not for the first time in Stuart history,
The entire affair is mired in mystery.

The King, as we know, enjoyed his racing.
He loved Newmarket. The air was bracing,
The countryside pleasant (if rather flat:
Jockeys, of course, didn't mind about that),
And the folk lively and agreeable.
What was completely unforeseeable
Was that the royal lodgings would burn down!
So Charles and brother James chose to leave town
One day earlier than contemplated.

Had they quit as first anticipated,
They'd likely have been assassinated.
For high on the London-Newmarket road
Stood the Rye House, just where the way narrowed.
The royals rode by, but a day too soon.
Twenty-four hours later, dead on noon,
That dreadful moment would have been their last –
Sitting ducks, the pair of them, riding past.
The plotters were wrong-footed. Damn and blast!
They'd missed their moment, chosen the wrong day.
To save their skins, some gave their mates away
And quite a number of the lesser prey
Were executed; others fled abroad;
Many, I suspect, were simply ignored.

Charles the Second and the Restoration

For Monmouth there was offered a reward:
Five hundred pounds. Put his dad to the sword?
The Duke denied it. You may rest assured –
Only my humble view, but there you are –
That James was unready to go that far.
In his father's eyes something of a star,
There was nonetheless now a price on his head.
So he kept a low profile, took to his bed,
And was lucky to live, it has to be said.

Not so the aforementioned Whigs – Russell,
Sidney and Essex. Charles showed his muscle:
All three were Exclusionists, true blue –
The Whig colours (this you probably knew).

Sidney was a republican, it's true.
No monarch! No King! That was his view.
He made no pretence of it. However,
There was no evidence whatsoever
Linking poor Sidney with the Rye House Plot.
Proof of involvement? Most certainly not!

Rhyming History

Sidney had the ill luck, take it from me,
To be tried by that arch-monstrosity,
Judge Jeffreys. His blood lust and savagery,
His malevolence, bullying, cruelty
And downright lack of decent humanity
(His sadism, indeed) were legendary.
Sidney managed his own defence most stoutly,
Yet his trial reeked of illegality.
Jeffreys conducted himself disgracefully,
With his waspish, ironic asides. 'Guilty'
Was the sure verdict – guilty of High Treason.
Justice and mercy were well out of season.
For there was no sniff of proof, no evidence
Of any Rye House link. The charge was nonsense.

Sidney met his end with stoicism,
True to his noble cause. Heroism
Is a word too readily bandied about,
But Algernon Sidney displayed it. No doubt.

William, Lord Russell, may well have sinned –
Sailed, I should say, rather close to the wind –
But the charge against Russell too, sadly,
Was illusory. He confessed, gladly,
To having deemed it lawful to 'resist'
The King (whatever that meant). To insist,
However, on his assassination
Was beyond the pale, an aberration.
Charles himself showed little consternation
When news were brought of the guilty verdict.
He might have pardoned Russell, but was strict.
"If I do not take his life," he averred,
"He will soon have mine." Patently absurd.
The evidence was riddled with hearsay.
His Lordship went to his death anyway.

It's said that his executioner, Ketch,
Badly bungled his beheading, the wretch.

Ketch blamed Russell for moving his body
At the wrong moment. I mean, really!
That's nothing, though, to Monmouth's death. Who knows
The truth of this tale? It took Ketch three blows
Before he threw down his axe. "I knew it!"
He's alleged to have cried. "I can't do it!"
Twice more he tried. Yet again he blew it.
He resorted to a knife. The Duke died
In awful agony. Oh, how they cried
(His enemies, I mean) – but with laughter,
James and his pals. Happy ever after?
Read on. I've lots of surprises in store.

Monmouth, however, survived two years more.
Whatever the panic caused (the furore)
By the Rye House Plot, the fortunate Duke
Earned little more than a royal rebuke.
Nevertheless, he was banished from Court.
He signed a confession (this the King sought),
But angered his father (surprised? I'm not)
By getting cold feet and relenting – the clot!
In exile, he carried on stirring the pot
With William, in Holland. Oh, I forgot,
A sad little postscript to the Rye House Plot:
The Earl of Essex, despatched to the Tower,
Slit his own throat. His career had turned sour.

Evelyn knew him slightly and called him "wise"
And "judicious". It came as some surprise
To find him championing Exclusion.
This caused no small measure of confusion
In the King's breast. Essex's dad, moreover,
Had died for King Charles the First, a walkover
When it came to Charles the Second's loyalty.
The family had stood up for royalty!
Essex served the King conscientiously
As Commissioner to the Treasury

And, earlier, for half a decade no less
As Lord Lieutenant of Ireland. I confess
To sympathising with Charles' sense of sadness.
When told of Essex's moment of madness,
He could scarcely believe that the Earl was dead.
He sat stock still. "I owed him a life," he said.

The King's declining years

The Rye House Plot was the last great event
To cause Charles concern. I shall rest content
To canter through his final year or so.
The Exclusionists, as now you know,
Had been routed. Monmouth (and his ego)
Were in eclipse. Whether he'd stooped so low
As to seek to assassinate the King
Is a secret of history. One thing,
However, which no one can now deny
Is that James, Duke of York, was riding high.
He'd been absent for over a decade
From the Privy Council. Charles, unafraid,
Restored his brother in May '84.   **1684**
The odious Test Act was still good law:
James had to relinquish, you may recall,
His splendid post of Lord High Admiral
Of the Navy. Now no one cared at all!
James took control again and men rejoiced,
As doubts and concerns were not even voiced.

The country was becoming, as I live,
Day by day largely more conservative.
Charles, in the twilight of his middle age,
Revealed himself as something of a sage.
Danby (and, before him, old Clarendon)
Had argued that peace would never be won,
At home, until religious dissent
Was snuffed out once and for all. What this meant

Charles the Second and the Restoration

(And the King knew it) was that Church and Crown
Should unite to put the dissenters down.
This they did. Enforcement was erratic –
Results were not exactly dramatic –
But hosts of dissenters, both Catholic
And Protestant, suffered persecution
By Tory magistrates: no solution,
Of course, to the problem in the long term,
But it did signal that the King stood firm
In the Church interest. Most men seemed content
To assume that this was also James' intent.

Thus it was that Charles the Second bequeathed
A strong monarchy to James. Tories breathed
With ease, as Monmouth waited and Whigs seethed.

The winter of '83/'84
Was the coldest on record. A wild boar
Was roasted on the Thames, I kid you not,
The ice several feet thick. Danby's lot

Rhyming History

Improved with his release from the dank Tower.
Sadly no longer the man of the hour,
Five years he had languished, the poor old soul.
Now into his fifties, time took its toll.

Yet he'd be back. In 1688
His role was pivotal. Titus Oates' fate,
Too, suffered a sea-change – his for the worse.
His ill-won pension from the public purse
Was first reduced, then stopped altogether.
A change in the political weather
Left him open to recrimination.
He was charged (amid some celebration)
With calling James, Duke of York, a traitor.
This notorious Catholic-baiter
Was tried by Judge Jeffreys and fined (mark this)
One hundred thousand pounds! Taking the piss?
I should say. Oates couldn't possibly pay.
Sent to gaol for ever and a day,
He was food for the Furies, come what may.

Under King James, Titus was tried again,
This time for perjury. Now, in the main,
I'd say the wretch deserved a good whipping.
Jeffreys, though, reckoned standards were slipping,
So sentenced him to be flayed from Aldgate,
Can you believe, all the way to Newgate
And then, two days later (such was his fate),
From Newgate to Tyburn. Should he survive –
And who, after that, could have stayed alive? –
He'd be treated to life imprisonment.
All at Judge Jeffrey's whim. No precedent.

Amazingly, Oates lived to tell the tale.
Although a rogue on a hideous scale,
I pity the poor devil. I'm no great fan,
But the snake bore his punishment like a man.

Charles took life gently, indulging himself
In his outdoor pursuits, in rude good health.
He enjoyed to the full his new-found wealth.
His 'indoor' interests (by which I mean
His mistresses, plural – rarely his Queen)
Continued, we're told, to monopolise
His lazier hours, to no one's surprise.
Nell and Louise were both still on the go –
Though never together, I'll have you know.

The King fought valiantly (and fought hard)
For James to succeed him. Yet scant regard
Did he have for his brother. He'd no trust
In his character. Support him he must,
As a royal Stuart, as next in line,
His heir, the King his father's son. Well, fine.
But Charles never really rated him
As monarch material. Far from dim,
James nonetheless was a perverse old fool,
Set in his ways and stubborn as a mule.
In short, the Duke lacked the temperament
For the rich subtleties of government.

Charles, in his wisdom, struggled tooth and nail
For his sibling, while suspecting he'd fail.
He left James his kingdom "in peace", he said,
Yet qualified his words: "When I am dead,
"I know not what my brother will do." Hah!
Some vote of confidence, but there you are.

Death of the King   1685

During the night of February the 1st,
1685 (a date forever cursed),
The King, according to reports, tossed and turned.
His man, Thomas Bruce, expressed himself concerned
That a huge wax candle that had brightly burned

Rhyming History

Extinguished itself without a breath of wind.
Ominous, he felt. The King was thicker-skinned
And, after a hearty supper of goose eggs,
Turned in. He had a pain in one of his legs
And spent, as I've hinted, an unsettled night.
The picture on the 2nd was none too bright.
His face was ashen, with bags under his eyes,
His tongue a dullish brown. It was no surprise
That his speech was slurred and his vision impaired.
The doctors were puzzled; young Thomas was scared.
But for what happened next they were unprepared.

Seated in his closet (his normal routine)
For his daily wash, Charles turned a shade of green,
Slumped forward and let out a terrible scream.
Dr. King (who heard it) rushed in with his fleam
(His blood-letting lancet), a pretty close shave,
And bled his royal majesty. This was brave.
He'd have been tried and hanged as a scurvy knave
Had the powers-that-be had a mind to it.
Charles' blood could only be drawn (and King knew it)
With the clear and specific authority
Of the Privy Council. Did he care? Not he!
This was a clear-cut, royal emergency.
The Council, it appears, agreed. King had grounds
For the bleeding. His reward: one thousand pounds.

The patient rallied, or seemed to, at least.
Then the torture began. Was he man or beast?
They shaved his head. All manner of blistering,
With red hot irons, they managed: 'clystering'.
The King was purged with enemas, cauterized,
Cupped, scalded – near bled to death. I'd be surprised
If a man half his age, in the rudest of health,
Could have lived a tenth of the time he did. By stealth
They drained him of his last pinch of energy,
As inch by inch he failed, a pity to see.

Charles the Second and the Restoration

Four days he suffered in this awful state.
James (bless him), fearful it might be too late,
Whispered in the King's ear: would he embrace
The Catholic faith? The Duke played his ace.

Charles' speech was weak, but his answer was clear:
"With all my heart! Lose… please… no time!" Oh, dear…
The King's chamber was bursting to the beams
With doctors, councillors, even (it seems)
With bishops, full five of them. "In your dreams"
Is one expression that springs to mind
For smuggling in a priest. Flying blind
Was James! What in God's name was he to do?
The room was packed with Protestants! He knew
Time was short. I'd have panicked, wouldn't you?

Yet James had trodden the Catholic path
Himself. The Earls of Feversham and Bath,
Both good Protestants, but trusted allies,
Could stay. The rest – to the bishops' surprise,

Rhyming History

Alarm and dismay – were dismissed. The King,
James informed them (those who were listening),
Lacked space and air. They should all retire,
No argument. Charles' burning desire –
This, quite obviously, not made public –
Was to die a God-fearing Catholic.
James hadn't much time. He had to be quick.

Strange as it might sound, the priest that he found
Was called Huddlestone. When Charles went to ground
After Worcester, what was the priest's name
Who sheltered him? You've forgotten it? Shame!
Father Huddlestone. Yes, the very same.

Now the King made a full confession
Of his sins. Forget the succession,
Forget politics, forget state affairs,
For subtle Death had crept up unawares.
Charles, the man, with fixed resolution,
And joy, accepted absolution.
He then received the blessed sacrament
Of extreme unction. He was content
To die a Catholic. His tearful Queen
Begged his forgiveness. What could she mean?
Charles begged *her* pardon, "with all my heart" –
The hardship she'd suffered… Where should he start?
He sought his brother's forgiveness as well.
James wept at his feet, it's moving to tell.

As for his mistresses, Louise and Nell,
They grieved from a distance. Nellie, I've read,
Yelled fit to burst. Around the King's deathbed
His children forgathered, his progeny
From six different mothers (allegedly) –
A humbling scene, most touching to see.
Monmouth was absent, ironically
(The most highly favoured), but only he.

Charles the Second and the Restoration

The King was sorry. He was so trying.
He apologised (there's no denying
His wit) for taking so long a-dying.

Evelyn notes that Charles took fine delight
In his "little spaniels". These, at night,
He suffered to snuggle into his bed.
The bitches gave suck (the puppies were fed)
Under the covers. It has to be said
That John was probably right to complain
Of the smell. It must have stunk like a drain!

Shortly before noon, then, on the fifth day,
Charles, it appeared, was ready to give way.
He commended his children to James' care,
Remembering, just, to wish his heir
A prosperous reign (some hope!). England wept.
James vowed (a promise I'm sure that he kept)
To take care of the mistresses, Louise
And Nell. After more than three centuries,
Few words have sounded more plaintive than these:
"Let not poor Nelly starve!" Their destinies,
Those of his women, could not pass Charles by.
With their fates secure, he could safely die.

Watch then as Charles the Second spreads his wings –
Most cavalier and colourful of Kings –
And soars towards the bosom of his Lord.
No Nelly there? I trust he won't get bored.

Bibliography

Maurice Ashley, *England in the Seventeenth Century* (Penguin, 3rd ed. 1961)

John Bowle (ed.), *The Diary of John Evelyn* (Oxford University Press, 1983)

Barry Coward, *The Stuart Age. England 1603-1714* (Pearson Education, 3rd ed. 2003)

Christopher Falkus, *The Life and Times of Charles II* (Weidenfeld and Nicolson, 1972)

Antonia Fraser, *King Charles II* (Phoenix, 1993)

Peter Furtado, *Restoration England* (Shire Publications, 2010)

Charles George, *The Stuarts. A Century of Experiment 1603-1714* (Hart-Davis Educational, 1975)

C. P. Hill, *Who's Who in Stuart Britain* (Shepheard-Walwyn, 1988)

John Miller, *James II* (Yale University Press, 2000)

John Miller, *The Stuarts* (Hambledon, 2006)

John Morrill, *The Stuarts* (in *The Oxford History of Britain*, ed. Kenneth O. Morgan – Oxford University Press, 2001)

Stuart Sim (ed.), *The Concise Pepys* (Wordsworth, 1997)

G. M. Trevelyan, *A Shortened History of England* (Penguin, 1959)

John Wroughton, *The Stuart Age, 1603-1714* (Longman, 1997)